ENERGY IS EVERYTHING – INCLUDING YOU

Reiki Smiles Creations

Alberta, Canada.

Copyright © 2020.

Text, poems, and drawings copyright ©
Hazel Butterworth
Cover images and sacred geometry images from Canva.

All rights reserved. No part of this book may be reproduced, copied, stored, or transmitted in any form or by any means - graphic, electronic, or mechanical, including photocopying, recording or information storage and retrieval systems, or other - without written permission from the publisher, except by a reviewer, who may quote brief passages in a review. Hazel Butterworth reserves the right to be identified as the author of this work.

All reasonable care has been taken in the preparation of this book. The information it contains is for educational purposes and is not meant to take the place of any medical care under the supervision of a doctor. Medicine has its brilliance too.

No expressed or implied guarantee as to the effects of the use of the recommendations can be given nor liability taken.
Any application of the ideas and information contained in this book is at the reader's sole discretion and responsibility.

HAZEL BUTTERWORTH

ENERGY is EVERYTHING, INCLUDING YOU

ENERGY IS EVERYTHING – INCLUDING YOU

Acknowledgments

I wish to dedicate this book to my husband, Dave, whose patience and support have enabled me to follow my heart to realize my dreams and live my passions.

I most especially want to express my love and gratitude for always being there for me as we navigated our way through life, and for being both my rock and my inspiration.

In addition, my heartfelt gratitude goes to all my family and friends who have also supported me along the way, even when they were not quite sure where I was headed with all my ideas, perceptions, or teachings.

With Heartfelt gratitude to everyone.

THANK YOU
I love you all.

HAZEL BUTTERWORTH

ENERGY is EVERYTHING, INCLUDING YOU

Hazel Butterworth

ENERGY IS EVERYTHING – INCLUDING YOU

Celebrate – "I AM ME"

I invite you to read this book slowly,
then revisit it again and again,
to deepen your awareness and understanding
of you, yourself, and your life.

Each time you refer to this book
you will resonate with something different,
depending on where you are at, within yourself,
and what you are experiencing in life.

I encourage you to journal
each time you visit the book and
see for yourself how you are evolving.

HAZEL BUTTERWORTH

This book is
packed full of
insights and inspirations
for you to
consider, ponder, explore,
implement, and integrate
into your own state of being.

It is written
as a practical
easy to read,
easy to navigate,
easy to comprehend
resource book.

Enjoy your adventure
to understanding
the many concepts
of who and what you are.

"ENERGY in MOTION"

EVERYTHING is ENERGY

including YOU

*"Everything is energy and that's all there is to it.
Match the frequency of the reality you want
and you cannot help but get that reality.
It can be no other way.
- Einstein*

*"If you want to find the secrets to the universe
Think in terms of energy, frequency, vibration "
- Nikola Tesla*

*"A mind that is stretched by a new experience
can never go back to its old dimensions."
— Oliver Wendell Holmes*

*"Your Energy vibes introduce you first.
Your Presence is felt by others
before you even say a word."
- Hazel Butterworth*

We are currently experiencing an

"ENERGETIC EVOLUTION"

"To "know" reality you cannot stand outside it and define it; you must enter into it, be it, and feel it."
- Alan Watts

"The mystery of life is not a problem to be solved, but a reality to be experienced."
- Alan Watts

"Everybody is a genius.
But if you judge a fish by its ability to climb a tree, it will live its whole life believing that it is stupid."
— Albert Einstein

There is no greater thing you can do with your life and your work than follow your passions –
in a way that serves the world and you.
-Richard Branson

ENERGY IS EVERYTHING
IN 3 EASY STEPS

"If I am the one creating my life"

1 - Where do I begin?

BEGIN WITHIN. P 11

2 - What must I know?

CONCEPTS EXPLAINED. P 33

3 - What must I realize?

BE AWARE OF
YOUR STATE OF BEING. P 169

HAZEL BUTTERWORTH

Stop Searching Elsewhere

The answers are within

PART ONE

If I am the one creating my life,

where do I begin?

It is simple...
BEGIN WITHIN.

ENERGY IS EVERYTHING – INCLUDING YOU

I AM -
ALL of ME

I AM -
past, present, and future,
ALL as ONE

I AM -
every version of me,
and every aspect of me,
ALL as ONE.

I AM that I AM.

HAZEL BUTTERWORTH

SOUL WHISPERS

Who am I?

*I AM THAT I AM.
I AM ME - but who is me?*

*I am not real, I am an illusion of me.
I am what I perceive myself to be.
I am the sum of all my experiences.*

*I am all of my decisions, thoughts, ideas,
memories, emotions, behaviors.
Every decision has brought me
to where I am today.*

*Every emotion has helped to sculpt me
Every belief and habit has created me
I have played many roles
I am ever-evolving, transforming*

*I am a Divine being of light
I am unlimited, eternal, infinite.*

*I am, who I am being, in this moment.
I AM. Consciousness, Love, and Light.*

I AM

Hazel Help
I felt inspired to write this book in the way it is written, to create more clarity, awareness, and understanding about the frequently asked questions of Who am I? Why am I here? What is my purpose?
Firstly, it is important to recognize the following
We are all Eternal, Infinite, Unlimited, Omnipotent (ALL Powerful) ENERGY Beings.

We are ALL part of Creation, we are all ONE with everything that is, ever has been, and ever will be.

We are part of a vast, invisible field of energy that contains all possible realities and responds to our thoughts, feelings, and choices.

We are all Source, Soul, Spirit, and Human.
All of these ENERGY bodies are part of the creative Force that consists of pure Love, Thoughts, Truth, and Consciousness.

We are here to experience life and evolve.
We experience this physical world that is bound by Universal Laws and limitations; a world of polarities, right/wrong, big/small; good/bad; judgment/criticism. EGO drives this duality within 3D living.

Aspects of ourselves show up in the people around us, just like mirrors, they reflect information about our true innermost selves.

We each have different perceptions, reactions, responses, thoughts, and beliefs, to every experience.

We are all unique, each with our own special gifts.

We were all born with Free Will, the freedom to think and feel as we choose; the freedom to form our own opinions; freedom to evolve or to stay stuck.
We all consist of variations of vibrations and frequencies of Light, Colour, and Sound.
Higher frequencies are fast like the speed of light. Lower frequencies are dense and appear solid.

Just like the moisture in the air,
that turns to visible clouds,
that turns to physical water,
that freezes to the solid matter as ice.
It is all moisture, presenting itself at different frequencies from invisible to physical form.
The same analogy applies to us,
*from **Consciousness Creation, or SOURCE** to **SOUL ESSENCE**, to **SPIRIT energy**, to the **PHYSICAL** dense energy form.*
Source, Soul, Spirit, Human.

We are the person that we are currently being; reacting or responding to whatever is happening in this moment of time; feeling what we are feeling; thinking what we are thinking; believing what we are believing; doing what we are doing.

Since birth, all choices and actions are based on previous experiences, programming, and learning.
We all play so many different roles during the day, constantly switching from one to another, then another, that we sometimes lose track of who our Real Authentic Self is, or what that looks and feels like. We then begin to ask ourselves, who am I?

Our purpose is simply to live life and evolve as we awaken conscious awareness and our inner wisdom.

We do this by becoming the observer.
The onlooker, who pays close attention to what is happening, in any given moment, with conscious self-awareness, and notices without any judgment.

We all have opportunities to learn and grow from each and every moment we experience.
Lessons may be repeated several times so that they can be approached and handled from a higher sense of awareness until they are completely embraced with love and acceptance, compassion, and understanding. Once achieved, there is no need to repeat these lessons or experiences. They are now resolved.

Love is the answer.
Love is the way, and Love is the solution.
It begins with self-love, love of life, love of others, and love of ALL living things. LOVE and BE LOVE.

Our purpose is to simply experience life.

IT JUST IS WHAT IT IS, no more no less.
It is simply recognizing, that in this moment, "THIS" is what is being experienced HERE and NOW. What some may call Karmic debt, is another opportunity to evolve by experiencing life from the duality perspective, from both sides of the equation, through this or many lifetimes. Our purpose is to transcend the world of 3D duality and emerge into our conscious awareness of TRUTH, the truth of what is behind the illusions of life.
As we evolve, we create our HEAVEN on EARTH,
We can live with LOVE, PEACE, and JOY, in BLISS and HARMONY, as life unfolds gracefully with ease.
This can be our HAPPY EVER AFTER life – NOW

WE ARE: -

Discovering how to become Self Aware
and Self Empowered, through Self Mastery.

Learning how to live life through
LOVE, COMPASSION, and UNDERSTANDING

Discovering how to take responsibility
for our own thoughts, words, and actions,
as well as for our own happiness and health.

Learning to UNLEARN or UNDO
the programming and limiting beliefs
imposed on us as children and young adults.

Awakening to the truth of who we are
and to realize that for ourselves.

Remembering how to love ourselves
and others unconditionally.

Realizing that we are responsible for
creating our own realities and outcomes.

Remembering who we are, how powerful,
how magnificent, and how gifted we are.
as the Creators of our own lives,
transforming our desires into physical realities.

Developing clarity and understanding
so that we can be Self Empowered
and FREE of the limits of the 3D duality world,
to enable us to live from a 5D perspective of
LOVE, PEACE, JOY, and BLISS.
and also experience beyond the 5D planes.

SOUL WHISPERS

I'm stuck

I'm here on the inside

longing to be on the outside

Wanting to step up, not ready to step out

Finding my feet, but unable to walk

Knowing my song, yet cannot sing

Filled with love, ready to share

Healed on the outside, scarred on the inside

Feeling my passion, bursting to expand

Trusting my Soul, even though EGO is present

Aware of the truth, still lying to myself

Ready to change, I must let go

If I do, who will catch me

Confined by fear, beliefs, and thoughts,

I am a prisoner to myself.

Soul whispers are the intuitive writings when I journal.

SOUL WHISPERS

I'm stuck where is the key?
Finding the key will set me free

The Key to Wellness
The Key to Happiness
The key to Success
The Key to Freedom
The Key to my Heart
The Key to Wisdom
The Key to Me

What does my key look like?

It could be as simple as
knowledge and understanding,
forgiveness, self-love
gratitude, compassion,
truth, awareness, courage,
letting go, allowing, accepting, embracing,
trusting my Soul, following my heart.

I AM the KEY
to set MYSELF FREE

ENERGY IS EVERYTHING – INCLUDING YOU

UNLOCK THE PIECES OF YOUR PUZZLE

Life is a Mystery.
We never know what is in store for us.
We have all spent time wondering who we are,
why we are here, and what is this life all about?

We sense there must be more to life,
more beyond the physical world,
more that we can do for ourselves,
more to our current existence.

We struggle to understand, comprehend, believe,
acknowledge, discover, admit, realize or accept.

We fear the unknown, the truth, pain, emotions,
feelings, thoughts, rejection, judgment, and ourselves.

We resist making changes, new ideas, and taking
responsibility for ourselves and the challenges in life.

We neglect ourselves when we always put everyone
and everything as a priority ahead of self-care.

You are the creator of your life.
Each decision you have made, each belief you have anchored, has brought you to where you are today. As your awareness evolves you will uncover more of life`s truths and realize for yourself, that you are your own catalyst for change, and that love is the answer to everything. You are responsible for your happiness.

Life is full of experiences, some are lessons, and some are simply opportunities to experience something firsthand so that you know what that something looks and feels like for yourself.
Each experience offers the potential to evolve or stay as you are, it is your choice, you have free will to make your own decisions.

It is important to learn how to connect to your own inner guidance so that your decisions can be made from the heart and soul and in alignment with your life plan, rather than from the EGO mind.

Your soul is part of The Divine, Intelligence,
Life Source Energy, GOD, Creator.
Your Soul is pure love, truth, and consciousness.
Your soul is your intrinsic 1st sense, not your 6th.

The soul is neutral and says "it is what it is"
whereas your Ego works from duality and is always playing both sides of what if`s or would have, could have. Ego is driven by fears and judgment.

Empowering Moments -
Do you know what you want in your life,
what your purpose is, what makes you happy,
what your giftedness is? Write it down and read it.

ENERGY IS EVERYTHING – INCLUDING YOU

Your Soul has your list (Life Plan) of things you wish to accomplish in this lifetime and is the purest of resources to go to, follow, and trust, if you wish to find the pieces of your own life puzzle.

It can be overwhelming when you recognize that something needs to change in your life but you do not know how or where to start.

It all begins and ends with YOU; it is YOUR Life.

*Self Awareness and Self Discovery are the **keys** to unlocking the Mysteries of your Life.*
*Self Journey is the **catalyst** for*
Self Realization and Self Actualization.
Self Empowerment and Self Mastery are
*the **results** of your efforts.*

You can Create your Blissful Heaven on Earth. your own "FREE to be ME." HERE and NOW

There are many inspirational books written that offer amazing insights into spirituality, health and wellbeing. Concepts are explained; insights are shared; science and theories are revealed. These books all have great content but without experiencing these for yourself, it can be more challenging to fully grasp them, put them into practice, or work with them effectively.

It is what you do with the knowledge you learn that makes the difference. It is how you integrate this knowledge and awareness into your own daily life. It is about being open-minded, willing to explore, willing to look closely at yourself, and willing to do the self-work.

"SELF WORK creates SELF WORTH - the best investment anyone can make is in themselves"

**It is possible to make sense of the NONE sense.
What may seem impossible or nonexistent
is indeed possible and does exist.**

What appears to be invisible becomes visible with self-awareness and realization. Science is catching up with the visionaries and intuitives to support their theories. Technology is now able to capture electromagnetic energies; studies and research are now proving some of the theories. Quantum physics, Neuroscience, and Epigenetics have all brought the None Sense into Sense, by proving we are all energy in motion.

Do you have to know all of the science?   NO
Is it enough to know that there is proof of how the Soul, Spirit, and Physical Body function?   YES.
Quantum physics explains that the subjective mind affects the objective world; the observer effect in quantum physics states that where you direct your attention is where you place your energy and that as a consequence you affect the material world.

**What you put your attention to you get more of,
be it good or not so good, you will attract more.
In Reiki, we work with the premise that
"Energy Follows Thought" and "Energy Works"**
With that in mind, if you focus on what you do not want, then you will create more of what you do not want. It is very easy for everyone to tell you what they do NOT want, yet it can be so difficult to express what they DO want. This is because they are so focused on their problems, rather than on their dreams and desires. It is easier to complain and criticize than to face the truth or take responsibility for oneself.

ENERGY IS EVERYTHING – INCLUDING YOU

Dr. Joe Dispenza talks about the thoughts we think of as being an electrical charge sent into the quantum field and the feelings that we generate magnetically draw events back to us. Always lead from the heart.

Quote: "Together how we think and feel produces a State of Being, which generates an electromagnetic signature that influences every atom in our world."

What you broadcast consciously or unconsciously is a magnet to what you invite into your life.
Many signature patterns exist for wealth, genius, and freedom. If you can change your state of being to match the potential of one of these, the possibility of it, is drawn to you, or you to that, magnetically and effortlessly. Life then becomes Easy Flow Living.
It is not enough to just think about what you desire, there also needs to be a connection to feelings in order to create the magnetic draw.
Both of these components must be in alignment or in agreement to manifest desires into the physical world.

Quote:" When you hold clear, focused thoughts about your purpose, accompanied by your passionate emotional engagement, you broadcast a stronger electromagnetic signal that pulls you toward a potential reality that matches what you want"
Dr. Joe Dispenza -
book: - Breaking the Habit of Being Yourself

Empowering Moments- Thoughts are the language of the brain, emotions are the language of the body, it is not enough to think something into existence, it has to be felt with the heart also.
Think, FEEL = Aligned = creates your REALITY.

Match the frequency
and it becomes your reality.

A person who wants to be successful cannot be successful if they currently feel like a failure.
You cannot feel two conflicting emotions at the same time. These mixed feelings will prevent your success. Some say fake it until you make it, if you tell yourself something often enough you will come to believe it to be true for you, but it will take a long, long time.

*The effective way is to **FEEL** the vibes.*

To be effective, align your thoughts and feelings to what you desire and the possibility will be drawn to you or you to it. Vibrate in that energy, and you will begin to experience it in your reality. It is important to be clear on what the end result will look and feel like, do not worry about how it will happen. The potential to become it will evolve for you. Be open to what is showing up in life and follow your intuition.

*What **do you** wish to **INVITE** into your Life?*

In the same way that we cannot solve a problem with the same thinking used to create it, we cannot create something new, with the same way of thinking and feelings currently being expressed. To bring about any changes in our external world we must first make changes within the internal world of our thoughts and feelings. FEEL the vibes of your desires with every ounce of your being and they will materialize. Everything already exists in the realms of possibilities. **Match that frequency and you will begin to experience it in your own reality.**

Visualization, imagination, and pretending play a large role in creating the life of your dreams. If you can imagine what it will look like, be like and feel like when you have what you desire, you begin to vibrate with that energy. Hold onto those visions and feelings.
SEE it - FEEL it – ATTUNE to it - BECOME it

When you imagine your dreams as your reality and feel it inside your heart as if it already exists, you are creating a connection or link to bring that future reality into the present. You are consciously weaving or knitting your dream into reality. There are no limitations to your imagination, anything is possible.

When you feel gratitude, you are vibrating on the frequency of Joy that something already exists. In truth, it already does exist in the realms of possibilities. Thank you, the more you are thankful, the more you will have to be thankful for.

When you feel the resonance, you are attuned to those frequencies. Think of a TV, when you TUNE INTO a specific channel, you experience what is on that channel. Imagine your desires are like choosing a TV channel and you are the one in charge of the remote. You get to decide what experience you wish to be immersed in. Imagine your dreams as limitless possibilities, all sitting there, waiting for you to simply tune into them. The Universe will always respond to your thoughts and feelings and create your reality accordingly, so it is essential to be aware of what frequencies you are vibrating with.

Abracadabra is a Hebrew phrase meaning "I create what I speak."

Knowing this to be true, you must always be consciously aware of not only the words you think; but also, the words you speak or write.

One of the first books that I read when I first began my search for truth was called, ***"The Game of Life"*** written around 100 years ago *by **Florence Scovel Shinn.*** Interestingly I have been gifted that book three times. When given the first book, my friend said "I read this book and thought of you, this is so you, you think as she does", I was honored. In her book, she explains a lot about how our words are all just energy; that our word is our wand; what we speak or think we create; that our words are magical; that it is important to choose words that have frequencies that are aligned with our intentions.

I resonate with a lot of authors and metaphysical philosophers from 100 years ago. What we teach about today is nothing new, except science is now supporting a lot of what we knew to be true but could not necessarily prove physically or logically to satisfy the Ego physical mindset.

It is important to begin listening with attention to the words and phrases you use, especially those that are repeatedly said over and over again, for they become so habitual that you no longer pay attention to them and no longer hear them. Active listening applies to listening to yourself, not just to others.

Empowering Moments
Try this for yourself, ask someone to repeat what they just said and most people cannot recall the words they have just spoken.

ENERGY IS EVERYTHING – INCLUDING YOU

RESPONSIBILITY - How we RESPOND in any moment, experience or situation is a direct result of all our previous experiences. Memories of past experiences, outcomes and consequences are all stored consciously and unconsciously. Patterns of behaviour emerge when similar situations arise.

These patterns become our traits, some of which can be detrimental to our current situation or relationships. AUTOMATIC REACTIONS are driven by subconscious memories, these are actions that require no conscious choice, they are merely a reflex reaction.

On occasion, it is helpful to have an automatic reflex reaction, but many times we react too quickly before we have the opportunity to choose how we wish to respond to what is happening in this NOW moment.

Similar to predictive text; as a scenario begins to play out, the brain is formulating and seeking familiarity from previous experiences which sets in motion a predictive action that prevents the opportunity to choose HOW you will respond.

PAUSE - a moment to check in with yourself.
BREATH - is essential, slow your breathing.
PRESENCE - is required, focus on this moment.
AWARENESS - is needed to choose a response.
CREATE - what you do in this moment will determine the outcome of this moment as it creates and evolves into the next now moment

We are ALL 100% RESPONSIBLE for everything we create, including our own HAPPINESS.

We are each 100% responsible for our own thoughts, words, and actions.
We all have the infinite ability to respond **TO** whatever is happening regardless of whatever **IS** happening, just so as long as we are present in the moment.

*Presence and Self Awareness
are key elements to
Self Empowerment and Self Realization.*

Responsibility is having the ability to respond.
Being responsible; is being accountable for yourself. Often, in childhood years, having that option of responsibility was not always possible, it was more about learning accountability and consequences, which were not always pleasant experiences. Fear and resistance, or pain became the emotions associated with accountability. Many children and even adults are afraid or hesitant of accepting or admitting any responsibility for themselves for fear of punishment, persecution, judgment, or repercussions.
If you understand you create your own reality, you can accept full responsibility for all that has ever happened in your life; the roles you have played, your contributions to situations; your actions and words; your choices and decisions; your outcomes.
When you move from automatic reactions to chosen responses, anticipation and excitement for new possibilities arise and doors begin to open.

Empowering Moments – RESPONSIBILITY
Do you take responsibility for your actions?
Do you respond or react to situations? Are you ready and willing to accept full responsibility for yourself?

ENERGY IS EVERYTHING – INCLUDING YOU

SOUL WHISPERS

We are ALL made of Universal Life Force.

We are simply energy *in continuous motion*
vibrating at different levels of frequencies.
We exist in this three-dimensional plane we call Earth,
which is governed by the Laws of the Universe and
experienced from duality or polarised perspective.

Everything is an experience *and*
we are the sum of those experiences.
We are here not just to learn but
to remember the truth of who we are.
We are here to Love completely,
deepen our understanding
live with compassion,
expand our awareness
and create Heaven on Earth NOW.

Our Soul is our pilot light from Source Light.
It is that twinkle in our eyes,
the radiance of our smiles,
the vitality of our aliveness.
It is the ignition of our motivation,
the brilliance of our ideas
the sparkle of our inspirations,
the catalyst and truth within
our LOVE-LIGHT that shines from within.
our 1st intrinsic sense, not our 6th sense
Shine your Soul LIGHT as brightly as you can.

Who are we?

I have come to the understanding that
I AM ME, I AM LOVE, I AM TRUTH,
I AM THOUGHT,
I AM DIVINE INTELLIGENCE
I AM ETERNAL, I AM PRESENCE.
I AM ONENESS. I AM.

*We are all connected energetically.
Physically, we appear as separate,
but in Spirit, we are ONE with ALL that is.
I AM in the universe, the universe is in me,
there is no separation. - unknown*

*"I AM he
as you are he
as you are me
and we are
ALL together."
- John Lennon*

SOUL WHISPERS

*"It is what it is
It is what it is not
It is
Full stop"*

*"Life is not as complicated
as you think it is."*

*"Life can be Easy Flow Living
and Effortless"*

*"Life happens FOR you
not TO you"*

*"Life is this everlasting moment,
ever-changing, ever-evolving"*

*"Life is for living, loving
laughing, and learning"*

HAZEL BUTTERWORTH

Explore and Discover

PART TWO

If I am the one creating my life,

what must I know?

Concepts Explained

ENERGY IS EVERYTHING – INCLUDING YOU

We are currently experiencing an
"ENERGETIC EVOLUTION"

"You, yourself, are the eternal energy which appears as this Universe. You didn't come into this world; you came out of it. Like a wave from the ocean."
- Alan Watts

Passion is energy. Feel the power that comes from focusing on what excites you.
- Oprah Winfrey

There is a vitality, a life force, an energy vibe, a quickening, that is translated through you into action, and because there is only one of you in all time, this expression is unique.
- Martha Graham

As soon as something stops being fun, I think it's time to move on. Life is too short to be unhappy. Waking up stressed and miserable is not a good way to live.
- Richard Branson

HAZEL BUTTERWORTH

ENERGY is EVERYTHING Including YOU

Believe in Yourself

I AM FREE to be ME

I AM the CREATOR of my life.

I AM INFINITE ENERGY

SOUL WHISPERS

The Magic is Within you.
YOU are
The Magician
The Wizard
The Genius
The Catalyst

The Creator is within you
You are
The Decision maker
The Dreamer
The Sculptor
The Designer

The Power is within you
You are
The Writer
The Editor
The Producer
The Star

You are
The light
The dark
And every colour
of the rainbow

You are
The sounds
The silence
The chaos
The calm

You are
The essence
The energy
The experiences
The expressions

You are
The thoughts
The emotions
The air that
you breathe.

You are
The steps
The dance
The songs that
You sing.

You are Magical
Let your Magic shine

ENERGY IS EVERYTHING – INCLUDING YOU

Empowering Moments
I~~m~~ possible
U~~n~~ able
I can ~~X~~

Definition of Empower -

inspire, authorize, enable, permit, warrant.

Changing attitudes from -

"I can`t" ... to .... "I can" – to...."I will" to... "I AM"

"Empowering Moments"

- giving yourself permission to action

a thought or a desire that motivates

and inspires you, even though it may feel

a little scary at the time.

It is the "CATALYST MOMENT"

that moves you forward to create changes

It is awakening your own Potential.

When you feel empowered -
you are able to accomplish your goals more readily,
you feel more confident and filled with vitality,
you have more control of your life,
you feel free of limitations,
you dare to face challenges
you have the agility to overcome obstacles,
you feel safe, knowing that you are capable
and that you can succeed,
you are motivated and more assertive,
you allow yourself to experience and embrace
whatever is happening NOW, this moment,
you surrender to the process.

Empowerment is about embracing changes and trusting your own inner guidance systems to take you in the best direction in life; it is about doing things that "feel right" for you and that makes you "feel good" on the inside; it is setting yourself free, no longer defined by others, you are free to be yourself; you can stand in your own power, stand tall, stand strong; it is putting trust in yourself, your abilities, your knowledge, and awareness, your choices; it is getting to know and understand yourself; it is overcoming fears and self-doubts.

Empowerment comes from feeling wholly connected to your "authentic self" the person you were born to be; it is the "knowing" of what is in alignment for your highest and best good; it is the certainty or willingness to make a decision trusting that however it turns out you can handle the outcome; it is believing in yourself. It is liberating yourself to be free of old paradigms so you can live your life in Easy flow and JOY.

LIGHT YOUR FIRE

Catalyst -

An agent which helps forward a
chemical reaction without itself
suffering any chemical change

Ignite -
Set on fire, kindle, heat to the temperature
at which combustion takes place

Ignition -
Setting on fire, firing of an explosive mixture of gases
using an electric spark.

Spark -
A small flash of light, liveliness, vitality, life,
intelligence, set alight, set-in motion.

HAZEL BUTTERWORTH

Become your own CATALYST

IGNITE the SPARK WITHIN YOURSELF
to EMPOWER YOURSELF
through SELF AWARENESS
and EMPOWERING MOMENTS.

SELF EMPOWERMENT
only happens when
YOU TAKE ACTION and
YOU PUT INTO PRACTICE
that which YOU are discovering
about YOURSELF.

Enjoy igniting your power,
Nobody else can do it for you.
YOU must do it FOR YOURSELF.

Are you ready to EMPOWER YOURSELF?

ENERGY IS EVERYTHING – INCLUDING YOU

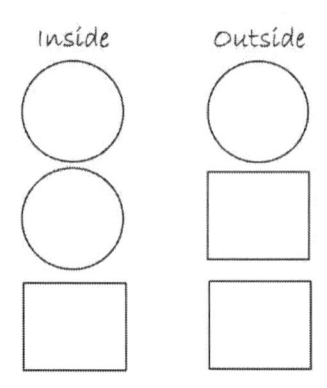

Inside   Outside

Be the Change you Want to Be

It is important to realize
that if you want to make changes in your life,
you must begin on the inside first.
If you wish to be a square, you must be square
internally for it to show up externally.
The outside world is simply
a mirror reflection of your inner world.
If there is chaos on the outside,
look within to see what chaos you are
experiencing in your own life and within yourself,
within your own world;
within your own thoughts and emotions.
Check in with your own contradictions,
perhaps you say one thing but do the opposite,
for example, I will stop eating a certain food,
then you eat some at the first opportunity.
If there is confusion on the outside
look within to see how you are confusing yourself,
maybe you have mixed emotions or
cannot make a decision, maybe you want to do
something but are too afraid to try.

When we want to change something in our own life,
be it where we live, our jobs, our friends, ourselves,
attitudes, or habits, we often start with a desire
or wish, then visualize what it may look and feel like.
We then begin to collect pictures, make a vision board,
or start saying affirmations to help create a focus on
the desired outcome. We think about it consistently.

What many people do not realize is that
WE must BE THE CHANGE.
We must be the catalyst that creates the action
to bring about the changes we desire.
Nothing happens unless we do something.
It is our own responsibility to action our desires.
What does that mean?
First, it means we have to be willing to change.
Second, have a clear detailed vision of
what the end result would look and feel like.
Third, start thinking, knowing, and trusting
it is already on its way or it already exists.
Fourth, take action steps to make it happen.
Each day take steps that will bring your desires closer.

Taking one step is better than no steps.
We do what we can with what we have now.

If we want to be a square, we can no longer
be a circle. When we change the inside first,
the outside will follow. If we want to be loved,
we must give love, starting with ourselves.
If we want to be appreciated, we must start
appreciating ourselves.
We create our own happiness in life.

ENERGY IS EVERYTHING – INCLUDING YOU

Explore and Discover

Self Realization - Actualization
Act of bringing into being - NOW
Act of becoming aware - NOW

Real
existing, factual, genuine, true, not imaginary.
Realistic
practical, clear-sighted, corresponding to facts.
Reality
state or quality of being true to life or fact.
Realize
perceive as a reality, understand clearly, become aware of, bring into being, cause to become fact.

Actual - existing at this present moment.
Actuality - real description of a current event.
Actualize - make actual; realize in action
Actually - in fact; at present now.
Perspective – a point of view, an attitude, or a particular way of regarding something
Perceive - see, apprehend, understand, observe, become aware of.

Perceived Reality is who or what we think we are in this moment in time. It is the illusion of what we believe to be real and the illusion of self-identity.
Perception – the process of becoming immediately aware of something, an insight, or an AHA moment.

Being Self Aware of "WHO I AM NOW" in this moment, in this physical world of existence, takes a willingness to look closely at oneself.
Observe what is currently happening; how you think, feel, talk, and behave. Look at your health and wellness, look at the people around you, the relationships you have with them, and with yourself.
Observe and Notice, simply become a witness.
This is just the beginning of Self Realization. Once you are aware of what currently exists, then you have choices to stay AS IS or EVOLVE... Your decision.

SELF REALIZATION
An act of becoming fully aware of
something as FACT/ TRUTH.
The fulfillment or achievement of
something desired or anticipated.
The act of accomplishing something.
The making or being made real,
of something imagined.
The fact or moment of starting to
understand a situation
The moment of achieving.

SELF REALIZATION is the ACT of
becoming completely aware of yourself.
SELF ACTUALIZATION is the ACT of
becoming your true AUTHENTIC SELF.

ENERGY IS EVERYTHING – INCLUDING YOU

Tipping the Scales

Evolve - To develop gradually and naturally.
When something evolves, it changes from a lower to a higher state of form. Latin word Evolvere "to unroll"
Evolved – A process that begins with conscious awakening. After the awakening, a person can no longer go back to the person they once were.

Ever-Evolving - As a person dives deeper into Self Awareness they are continuing to evolve.
Evolution - the process of evolving; gradual development; progressive series of changes; cumulative change in characteristics.; occurring through generations. Evolutions happen where you are, you do not have to go anywhere, or get from A to B. All you need to do is let life flow and unfold itself.

Evolution is always happening in this moment, the NOW moment, which is the ETERNAL NOW.

THE TIPPING POINT - WHAT IS YOURS?
What has to happen in order for you to change?

What makes you finally decide that you cannot continue the way you are; that the way you think or feel is not healthy; that your actions are hurting others and yourself; that the way you live is creating anxiety, or this is all there is unless you change?

What is the last straw that creates your incentive to seek changes within yourself?

It may be that you simply say -
Enough is Enough, I cannot take anymore.
I am not happy, or I deserve to be happy.
I have to change my ways, thoughts, or actions.
It may be fear-driven -
I am afraid I will lose my job.
I am afraid my marriage will not last.
I am afraid to lose a friendship.
I am afraid it will be too late to start.
It may be goal or purpose-driven -
If I am to reach my goal, I must change something
I need to devote more time to myself.

Sometimes it is a comment that triggers a reaction in you; or a realization that if you do not make the changes, nothing changes. It may be reward-driven and you reap the benefits personally.
Whatever the reason you feel the desire to change something about yourself, do it from a place of LOVE.

Your incentives will help drive your motivation, dedication, and commitment, to create the changes you need to make for you to EVOLVE and become the next version of YOU.

Empowering Moments

You have the power to change your life
You have the power to Reprogram yourself
You have the power to Let go of Anxiety,
Fear, Doubts, old beliefs, old programming.
You have the power to Create and Manifest
the life you wish to live each and every day.
You have the power to invite Happiness
into every day that you live.
YOU have the POWER to EVOLVE

First, you must be open to all possibilities,
have an open mind, be willing to explore and discover,
be willing to learn, as well as be willing to unlearn.
Second, you must become Self-aware,
as you become more self-aware you will become Self
Empowered, this is where the magic comes to light.
Third, see the end results, surrender, and trust the
universe will conspire to match your vision.
As you Empower yourself, changes will happen and
you will be able to make life-changing decisions for
yourself comfortably, and confidently.
Life will become EASY FLOW LIVING

LOOK / SEE / CHOOSE / BE = EVOLVE

LOOK – Self Analysis /Soul Self
Who /What are you? - A Soul experiencing life.
Be willing to look beyond the physical.
Be willing to look at every aspect of yourself.

SEE – Self Awareness /Self Reflection
Conscious awareness of Self and Higher Self.
I am me, the sum of my experiences. See and
understand yourself; your behavior, thoughts,
programming, emotions, dreams, and intuition.
Be clear on who you are currently being.

CHOOSE – Self Empowerment
Making conscious choices for yourself,
that are in alignment with your SOUL truth.
Creating your life of happiness and bliss.
Choose what you keep and what you release.

BE – Self Mastery /Self Realization
Walking your walk, and talking your talk.
Living from heart, allowing, embracing,
with compassion and understanding.
Being the best version of yourself.
Living in alignment with your Soul.

YOU are the creator, scriptwriter, editor,
producer, and main character in your life.
It is your journey to remembering your TRUE SELF.
Whatever you envision already exists, match the
frequency, be willing to step into that version of you.

ENJOY the EXPERIENCES along the way.
Self Mastery = Realize /Actualize /EVOLVE

ENERGY IS EVERYTHING – INCLUDING YOU

Believe in Yourself

Experience. Knowledge, understanding, or practical wisdom gained from what one has observed, encountered, or undergone.

Experience. Something that happens, which creates an awareness of how it affected you.

Experience is obtained from doing, seeing, hearing, or feeling, using our physical senses, our conscious awareness, and our intuition.

Experiences in life help shape the way we view ourselves and the world around us.

Experiences often define who we become and how we live our individual lives.

Experience. Been there, done that myself.

Life is a series of experiences, one after another. Awaken and witness your own experiences.

Every moment, every day, you are experiencing the physical world through your conscious and sensory awareness, you are continually processing everything that is happening NOW, in this moment, on all levels of your being. Every experience impacts you and influences you, and how you interpret or process these experiences depends entirely on you,

Based on previous experiences you may have a preconceived idea of what the current or next experience may look and feel like. This may prevent you from doing something, or it may motivate you to have another similar experience again and again. **No Experience is ever wasted.**

"I believe that everything that happens to you is the greatest thing that could ever happen to you. Everything — because that is exactly how the universe works. It gives you whatever you are in alignment with, and it's all designed to work on the weakest link you have." Jim Carrey –

> ***Empowering moments -***
> *What is your weakest link?*
> *What are you in alignment with?*

Being present NOW, this moment; is being fully present with the experience; awake, aware, engaged, and open to the potential and possibilities. This NOW moment is where Life happens, not the past, not the future, NOW. **This NOW moment is continually evolving.**
It is, this present moment, always in motion, which creates the continued momentum to live a
MOMENTOUS LIFE.

Take the First Step - Onwards, Upwards

RESISTANCE - That which we resist persists.
When we resist something, we deny ourselves, we prevent ourselves from achieving what we desire, we hold back, we find excuses, we limit ourselves, we diminish ourselves, we abuse ourselves.

What does resistance look and feel like?
Perhaps it is driven by fear, fear of not only failing but perhaps fear of succeeding. Perhaps it is not accepting possibilities; not realizing the full potential; not being willing to change or to stand in your truth; fear of being judged or criticized; fear of the unknown; or doubting yourself. Resistance makes life harder. When you resist, your body fights against what is happening, it tightens up, restricts blood supply, tension, fear grabs a hold of you and the chemistry in your body becomes toxic. Toxicity creates illness.

Resistance - can be a belief that is driving you; you are not worthy; you do not deserve; you live in the wrong part of town; no one in your family has ever achieved that. It could be a memory of trying before but not succeeding. It could also be fear of succeeding.

**Whatever the resistance,
it will persist until you make peace with it.**
It may be a belief that good things only happen to others; I am not good enough; I am not clever enough; I have money but I always lose it; I can`t believe; I always lose; I`ll never get the opportunity.
One phrase a client said was "I have never-ending failed relationships" WOW never-ending? How is this person ever going to have a relationship when at the core level the belief is "I have never-ending failed relationships" there is no possibility of ever succeeding or having a relationship working out with this much resistance. He thought he would be forever single.
We rephrased that statement (RATS) he accepted that - UP UNTIL NOW, that had been the perception. Up until now, it appeared as if they were never-ending. We changed it to - "I AM, able to have flourishing successful relationships." This changed the dynamics and perception of this belief to " anything is possible " He let go of resistance, next relationship blossomed.

Resistance is a choice, when we let go of it,
we move from the **IDEA of Infinite Possibilities,**
to **EXPERIENCING Infinite possibilities.**
Every possibility already exists, choose the ones that are your heart's desires and simply **step into them.**
We can bring ideas into reality; dreams and desires to fruition; goals to achievements; wishes to experiences; all through our own Conscious Creation.
Remove the resistances and allow life to flow.

> *Empowering moments - RESISTANCE*
> *What are you currently resisting?*
> *What are you really afraid of?*

I LOVE Me ♡

LOVE Every Aspect of Yourself

ACCEPTANCE BEGINS WITH ME

Accept - receive willingly something given or offered
- to consider or hold as true, exactly as it is.
- tolerate or accommodate oneself and one's reality
- to endure without protest or reaction, no good/bad
- to agree to undertake (a responsibility)

Accepting – amenable, open-minded
- able or willing to accept something or someone
- inclined to regard something or someone with acceptance rather than with hostility or fear
- means valuing and tolerating differences
- having inner nonresistance, being ok with what is.

Self Acceptance – being ok with who you are being.
- accepting ALL your attributes, positive or negative.
- embracing every part of yourself, every aspect, every trait, characteristic, strength, or weakness.
- to be self-accepting, is to feel satisfied with who you are, regardless of past choices, beliefs, or behaviours.
- to be without judgment or criticism of yourself.

My "Freedom 55" was FREE to be ME.
This is who I am. I accepted this was ME.
I LOVE WHO I AM and WHO I AM BEING

"Accept – then act. Whatever the present moment contains, accept it as if you had chosen it. Always work with it, not against it." – Eckhart Tolle

SOUL = Allow, Surrender. **EGO =** Resistance
There are two ways out of a problem: accept what's happening, flow with it, and choose a solution to move through it, or fight against it, resist it and struggle against it. Accepting "what is", is accepting that life is happening "FOR" you, not "To" you (victim), and that each and every experience is helping you to learn, grow, and evolve. Acceptance creates freedom.
Accepting what has happened, even though it may have been painful, will create opportunities for self-healing and understanding. You cannot change what has happened, but when you accept that it did happen, you now have an opportunity to explore and discover what that experience was showing you. (RATS p 114)
Accepting your reality for what it is, does not necessarily mean you like that reality; that you agree with your own behaviour; or condone anyone else's behaviour; or that you must agree to everything. Think of it as simply acknowledging its existence.
Unconditional Self Acceptance is knowing yourself and still being comfortable with who you are and who you are being. Reaching this level of awareness may take some time, as you will need to navigate your way through your Self Judgement, and be willing to look closely and deeply at yourself, your past thoughts, emotions, beliefs, behaviours, and experiences.

Empowering Moments -
Ask yourself - Am I accepting of myself?
Do I accept that I choose ALL MY experiences?

UNCOVERING TRUTHS

We often feel there is more to life, and begin searching for that something we feel is missing but as we uncover life`s truths, we ultimately discover that the innate truth has always been there, ready and waiting to be uncovered, recognized, and acknowledged.

Awakening to the truth of who we really are, pure love, Divine intelligence, infinite eternal energy with limitless possibilities and potential, can be a gentle effortless unfolding process. We are far more powerful than we realize. We are magnificent creators of our lives. With ease and grace, we can align to our Soul's truth as we continue to learn, grow, and evolve.

Three inspired intentions or mantras -
"My life is synchronicity in motion "
"Everything flows effortlessly with Ease and Grace"
"I live my life divinely and consciously"

Living your Soul truth makes life so much easier. It is knowing who you are at the core level of awareness, understanding your character and traits, and recognizing when you are being truthful, especially to yourself. " Your body does not lie; it knows truth instinctively and will respond accordingly. Muscle testing is a good way to ask your body questions

Living your Soul Truth requires you to speak your truth from your heart; to speak from a place of love even when it may seem difficult or fearful.

Living your Soul Truth is following your heart's desires; living passionately doing what you love to do; honestly with integrity, freely, and abundantly.

Your Soul knows your truth, has your blueprint, has your life plan, and is your True Authentic Self.

Home Truth - when someone says something and you know it to be absolutely true for you, it can sometimes "hit home" in a good way or not-so-good way.

Your soul always knows the truth.
Sometimes you will get goosebumps. I know for me, when I say something or feel something that is an absolute truth for me, I get a sudden shiver, and the **"TRUTH BUMPS"** (goosebumps) show up.

Empowering Moments - TRUTH
What is absolutely true for you?
How do you recognize when you are in truth?
Are you true to yourself?
Are you aligned to your Soul, your soul blueprint, your Soul Plan, your Soul Purpose?

UNDERSTANDING

Understanding is when we can comprehend and accept something, its an intelligence, a knowing.

When we come to an understanding, it is an agreement, that the knowledge we have acquired, we comprehend, we grasp, and we get it.

Acknowledging that we understand helps to foster relationships and opens communication.

As we evolve, we come to understand ourselves and life more deeply, with a higher level of conscious awareness and compassion.

To understand someone or something does not mean that we must agree, it simply means we are aware of another perspective, perception, or opinion. We acknowledge everyone has their own interpretation of words and experiences and that no two people have the same interpretation of an experience.

As we explore and discover we begin to understand our feelings and emotions, our reactions and responses, our behaviours, and our own selves.
We begin to understand how we have allowed emotions and Ego to control us; how our fears have debilitated us; how others have influenced or controlled us; and how powerless we had become.
Understanding is a choice, without it, we continue to function in our lives without ever knowing how we created it, how to deal with it or how to change it.

> **We understand**
> **what we understand**
> **in this moment,**
> **now,**
> **based on**
> **what we have learned,**
> **up till now.**

When we get it - we are free of confusion.
When we understand - it no longer eludes us.

When we get it - life is simpler
When we understand - we are Empowered.

When we get it – we are no longer attached to it
When we understand – it dissolves itself.

Empowering Moments – UNDERSTANDING
Do you understand yourself?
Do you understand your emotions and feelings?
Do you comprehend how you create your own happiness?
Do you understand your relationships?

ENERGY IS EVERYTHING – INCLUDING YOU

SURRENDER TO THE EXPERIENCE

Surrender
Yield oneself to; give up to a higher power.
Cease to resist; Embrace; Allow; Accept.
When you surrender to an experience or an
emotion, you stop trying to prevent it, resist, fight
or control it, you simply allow and embrace the energy.

Going with the flow is a smoother experience.

Surrendering to yourself means living your truth,
allowing your higher intuitive self to guide you,
embracing each experience that is presented,
accepting that everything is as it is meant to be,
it is all in your Life Plan, and trusting in yourself.

Spiritual surrender is surrendering to life as it is
and to simply be present in the moment and trust that
everything will work out for your highest good.
Nothing has to be forced, everything will unfold in
Divine timing, according to your Life Plan.

Michael A Singer, *The Untethered Soul and The Surrender Experiment are two excellent reads*

Surrender to the Experience is not giving up, not giving in, or being defeated, it is simply choosing to go with the momentum rather than resisting what is happening. It is being at peace, willing to allow, embrace, accept and experience the moment fully. It is trusting that this experience is perfect for you.

Your Soul always has your back, you are safe.

Allow
Permit, acknowledge what is happening;
allow feelings and emotions to rise to the surface.
Embrace
Welcome the unknown, and approach with love, kindness, compassion, understanding, & courage.
Accept
it is what it is, no more, no less. Stay with the facts, accept responsibility, admit, and agree. Be at peace with what is happening, your decisions, your choices.

Go with the flow,
see where it leads; discover what this experience is showing you. "I wonder what I will experience"

Spiritual -
surrender to the natural order of life, feel connected, and trust your SOUL and SOURCE to guide you.

> *Empowering Moments – SURRENDER*
> *Are you willing...*
> *to trust hat life is happening FOR you?*
> *to surrender and go with the flow?*
> *to allow, embrace, or accept?*
> *Have you experienced this easy flow?*

ENERGY IS EVERYTHING – INCLUDING YOU

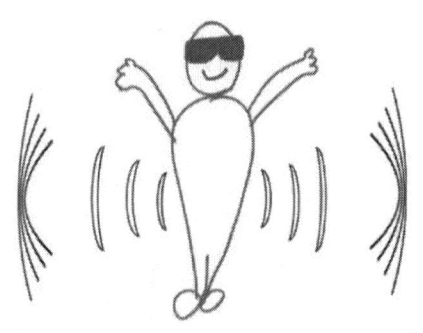

Raise your own Frequency Vibrations

We are all ENERGY in MOTION
Energy does not stop it only changes form.
It cannot be destroyed, only transmitted, transfered or transmuted into another form.
There is no beginning, no end,
only motion as it eclipses itself.

MOISTURE - CLOUDS - WATER - ICE
Moisture emerges from invisible to visible.
As moisture changes its frequency it changes its appearance, it forms tiny particles that create CLOUDS, as the frequency lowers and the vibrations slow down, those particles become liquid as WATER, when they slow down, even more, they create the appearance of a solid, like ICE. It is all still MOISTURE that changes form depending on its frequency.

We are Universal Light Source Energy (moisture) that has been transformed into the appearance of solid physical bodies, (ice) yet we are all still SOURCE.

We each vibrate at different frequencies.
We each have our original Soul Frequency vibration that is unique to us, plus or minus the frequencies of thoughts, emotions, and behaviours.

Universal Energy or Light Source Energy

We are Light - Colour and Sound frequencies
We are Consciousness - Thought frequencies
We are Love - Emotion frequencies
We are Infinite, Limitless, Intelligent, Eternal Energy. We are Love and Light.
These infinite intelligent energies all interact, integrate, and influence each other continuously, nothing is solid, it only appears to be solid when it has dense energy.

Humans are the **VISIBLE** combination of these energies that show up as the appearance of a solid physical body. We express thoughts and emotions through our words, feelings, and deeds, in the form of verbal language, body language, and behaviours.

Our thoughts and emotions influence who we are being in any given moment. How we respond to thoughts and emotions, creates choices, which we then put into motion as behaviours. How we behave is our current STATE of BEING.
For anything to manifest in the physical world, it is first created by thoughts and feelings, which then instigate the actions, that then create your reality.
Think, Feel, Create (action) = Perceived Reality

Empowering Moments -
Think of an idea, what do you wish to create?
Visualize what that will look and FEEL like for you.
Imagine you are living that NOW, see it in your mind's eye and feel yourself doing it NOW.
The potential exists, it is waiting for you to make the connection to it and live it for yourself.

ENERGY IS EVERYTHING – INCLUDING YOU

Live in the Light

**We are Light, Colour and Sound
As "Light Beings", we come from
"The Light" and return to "The Light"
then emerge again as another
SOUL SPARK OF LIGHT.**

As we blink in and out of existence, we are always in motion, experiencing, evolving, and transforming. When holographic rainbows appear, we see them but we cannot touch them, because they are not physical. We too are holograms of light, we vibrate so slowly that we become visible, physical human beings.
White Light, visible Light, when directed into a prism, splits into 7 rainbow colours, each colour vibrating on its frequency. We have 7 main energy centres called Chakras which filter all the individual colour frequencies into our energy body, they are then transmitted along the energy pathways (meridians) which then communicate with our physical bodies.
Just like a printer needs full ink cartridges, we need to keep our energy centres topped up for us to be healthy and to function effectively and efficiently.

HAZEL BUTTERWORTH

**Colour is visible Sound,
Sound is audible Colour,
the only difference is the frequency.**
Colour is a sound frequency that is so high-pitched that we cannot hear it with our physical ears. Dog whistles are a good example of this. Sound traveling fast becomes the light that we can see. Light travels faster than sound as we are aware when there is lightning and thunder, we see the flash before we hear thunder.
A gentleman who could only see black and white used sounds to determine colours.
He had a camera fixed to his head which would pick up images of what he was looking at, then a computer would lower the frequencies of the colours to audible sounds. Instead of painting by numbers he painted colours by sounds. Every sound has its own colour.
The sound of your own voice is magical; it has a resonance that vibrates in every fiber of your being. Place your hands over your ears and listen to your voice, you will feel the vibes for yourself. Vocal toning of the vowels, a, e, i, o, and u is very effective to do.

Every organ, body part, or system in your body has its own optimum frequency which can be restored through exposure to colour and sound. Sunlight, white light, is essential for promoting good health. Our bodies are intuitive and know exactly what colour or sounds it needs to restore its own optimal frequency. Sunlight, water, and breathing are the most important ingredients for us to survive.
Darius Dinshah *(1873-1966) was the inventor of the Spectrocrome system (colour lamps) used in colour therapy today. His book – "Let there be Light" is a great resource, based on his scientific studies.*

THE "FEEL GOOD" FACTOR

**Nobody knows HOW you feel,
Nobody can FEEL what you feel
YOU are the only person who can
FEEL and KNOW what & how YOU FEEL**

EMOTION - is Energy in MOTION. The unconscious mind is the source of emotions and the emotion itself is an aspect of it. Emotions set thoughts, feelings, and actions into motion, as an expression of that emotion.
FEELING - is the conscious awareness of the effects emotions have on the body.
WE FEEL the EMOTION we are experiencing in any given moment, it shows up and is demonstrated as a behavioural response in the physical body.
Emotions and feelings create your biochemistry.
Just like we cannot see the wind, we cannot see emotions. We only see the effects they have on the physical body, which is demonstrated by a person's physical actions. It is like falling in Love, you just know when you love someone by how you are feeling, and your actions will then demonstrate those feelings.

The **EMOTION of LOVE** creates an amazing **FEELING** inside you that lights you up as it radiates from every cell in your body and creates your glow. **LOVE** can make you feel alive, excited, and on top of the world. **LOVE** can motivate and inspire you.
LOVE can help you be more creative or determined.
The more you FEEL GOOD, the more you release your resistance and the more you allow that which you desire and are passionate about, to show up.
Too often, people have closed their hearts for fear of being hurt. They put up walls and barriers to prevent experiencing painful emotions. What they do not realize is, that if their heart is closed, they cannot experience any emotion at all, everything is shut off, nothing comes in or out, and love is absent.
Emotions can become trapped and stuck. It is difficult to motivate yourself or BE HAPPY if you have no feelings, are numb inside, and Happiness is absent.
EVERYTHING IS LOVE or
LACK of LOVE - the separation from love.
I strongly encourage you to do more of what makes your **HEART SMILE and FEELS GOOD** inside, **LIGHTS** you up, **MOTIVATES,** and **INSPIRES** you. Do things you **ENJOY** doing, whatever works for you to bring a smile to your face and a warm fuzzy feeling inside you. Be with people you enjoy being with, and go to places you enjoy. Focus on JOY, kindness, compassion, empathy, and love. All these emotions create a chemical response within your body that directly impacts your health and well-being.

> ***Empowering Moments -***
> *What makes your heart smile?*
> *What makes you FEEL GOOD inside?*

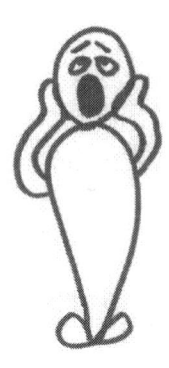

UNPLEASANT OR UNWANTED EMOTIONS

When unwanted emotions show up, we often have no desire to express them, experience them, or even acknowledge them.

Our coping mechanism is to deny them, ignore them, hide them, suppress them, or shove them so far deep down within ourselves never to see daylight again.

Perhaps it's not the time to cry; perhaps we perceive it would be a sign of weakness; perhaps we do not want to let someone know how we truly feel because we do not wish to hurt them; perhaps we do not know how to express our feelings in this moment and so we choose to hold on to them or try to hide them.

Whatever the reason, suppressed emotions will be stored in the physical body until they can be dissolved or released. **These trapped frozen emotions cause dis-ease as they fester and become toxic energy within the body.** Eventually, they will eat away at you or deplete you of your vital life force energy.

FEAR and ANXIETY

FEAR can be very debilitating. It can prevent you from doing the very things you wish to do. When fear shows up it is important to pause and look closely at what the true underlying fear is. A fear of heights could be the fear of falling and getting hurt.

Eckhart Tolle in his book ***The Power of NOW*** *explains fear – quote "The psychological condition of fear is divorced from any concrete and true immediate danger. It comes in many forms: unease, worry, anxiety, nervousness, tension, dread, phobia, and so on.* **This kind of psychological fear is always of something that might happen, not of something that is happening now.** *You are in the here and now, while your mind is in the future, this creates an* **anxiety gap.** *If you are identified with your mind and have lost touch with the power and simplicity of the Now, that anxiety gap will be your constant companion. You can always cope with the present moment, but you cannot cope with something that is only a mind projection - you cannot cope with the future.*
Fear seems to have many causes. Fear of loss, fear of failure, fear of being hurt, and so on, but **ultimately all fear is the ego's fear of death, of annihilation.** *To the ego, death is always just around the corner."*
Unless you are in imminent danger,
    fear is a psychological fear, in other words,
       it is only in your mind, it is not real.

> **Empowering Moments -**
> What are your true fears?
> What are you afraid to do, be, think or feel?

ENERGY IS EVERYTHING – INCLUDING YOU

Allow and Acknowledge All Emotions

EXPRESSING an EMOTION is how a person relays how they FEEL in any given moment.

There is no right or wrong, it is what it is.
In this moment I feel angry, in this moment I feel excited. The key is not to be confined by those emotions that do not bring you JOY; not to deny them; not to store them; and not to ignore them.
Express emotions freely and constructively.

If you only feel anger, guilt, and resentment,
then that is all you see in front of you and you get stuck in that pattern. What you project, reflects back to you, so if you are always angry then life gives you more to be angry about, and you will continue to meet every experience with anger.

If you are always angry, annoyed, or disgruntled, you wear yourself down, to the point that your body begins to respond to the lower frequencies. The lower frequencies promote illness and disease. Anger and worry eat away at you, guilt wears you down, hate destroys you, and anxiety disrupts your flow of energy.

Scientific research is now able to prove that emotions stored in the body do contribute to sickness.
There is a definite correlation between health and happiness, sickness and sadness.
Very often we are taught not to show emotions, perhaps it's not the time or place, perhaps it would be a sign of weakness to cry. This has caused many people to ignore, deny or simply push emotions back, which is not healthy.
Experiencing ALL emotions is healthy.
How you process, deny or store those emotions will determine your health and happiness.
Where an illness shows up in the body gives the person a clue for what to look at within their own lifestyle, attitudes, behaviors, and relationships. A book called "***The Secret Language of the Body***" by **Inna Segal** is an excellent resource for finding the correlation between emotions and illness. The book is divided into sections - body parts, physical ailments, emotions, colour, and body systems so that it is easy to navigate and find the clues to understanding what your body is trying to tell you. Your body never lies.

It is not always easy to express emotions or process them, but it is essential for good health that we learn to acknowledge them and work through them, especially the emotions with the energies of the lower frequencies.

> ***Empowering Moments*** -
> *Pause, breathe, allow the emotion,*
> *sit with it, experience it, acknowledge it,*
> *let it flow. As you continue to breathe,*
> *it will dissolve itself as it moves through you.*

THE NEGATIVITY FACTOR

Negativity is not a bad thing, it is simply a negative response to what is happening.

Just like a coin has two sides, together they are ONE COIN. Negativity and positivity are two energies that Co-exist together as interpretations of all experiences.

Most people view negativity as bad and positivity as good, they strive to always see the positive side of things. Trying to be positive all the time creates a lot of disharmonies and denies a person the opportunity to express themselves truthfully and honestly.

Holding in negative energy is not healthy.
Simply recognize what you are experiencing, without judging if it is good or bad. It is simply your response to an experience. Negative responses are a way of letting you know to be curious about your reaction and to look more closely at the situation or experience.

**POSITIVE OR NEGATIVE, IT IS WHAT IT IS
... A RESPONSE TO AN EXPERIENCE.**

POSITIVE OR NEGATIVE

The importance here is about navigating each/every experience and realizing whether that experience is impacting you positively or negatively.
There is no right or wrong, both are expressions and interpretations of emotions felt in that moment.

It is possible for positive outcomes to evolve from negative experiences.

Fallout in a relationship can bring new awareness and understanding that brings two people closer. An illness can encourage a person to eat healthily and exercise more diligently. A cancer scare can be a huge wake-up call to resolve emotional issues that have been stored in the body. A negative comment can inspire you to look more deeply within yourself.

A negative experience can inspire you to make changes in your lifestyle or to spend time exploring an inner self-journey to understand what the lesson is.

When a person is too much, either way, all negative with no positive, or all positive with no negative, that person becomes out of balance and out of sync.
A battery requires both negative and positive charges to work effectively, and so do humans, as we too are made from the same positive and negative forces.

Our role is simply to be "PRESENT and AWARE" of how we are feeling, what we are thinking, how we are responding and how each experience is impacting us. Self-awareness is the key to understanding ourselves and empowering ourselves.

ENERGY IS EVERYTHING – INCLUDING YOU

RESILIENCE

The power to return to original condition; the capacity to recover quickly from difficulties; toughness.
The process of adapting well in the face of adversity, stress, or trauma. Ability to remain true to self.
Life throws curve balls sometimes.
Things such as sickness, trauma, tragedy, and threats are significant sources of stress. Things such as family or work relationship problems can cause stress.
How you cope with or navigate through them will determine how quickly you recover from them and how soon you can move on from them. **To be resilient** a person needs love, forgiveness, compassion, and understanding as well as a desire to be healthy.
Life is filled with ups and downs, twists and turns, uncertainties, and unknowns. Being able to trust your innermost self is essential to rebound quickly.
Rebound - Bounce back; renew energy; come back to the pre-existing state; restore equilibrium.

> *Empowering Moments*
> *Recall a time when you rebounded well, how did you manage to do that?*

To be Resilient, it is essential to recognize and understand these parts of SELF, and to know which part creates resistance and which creates resilience.
SOUL SELF is neutral, with no agenda, no judgment. Your soul is pure love, acceptance, and compassion. Your soul will always guide you to your truth and keep you on your soul path. Your soul is honest with you, embraces every experience, and encourages you. Your intuition and gut instincts are driven by your Soul. Trust your Soul implicitly as your soul whispers gently. Higher Self is a term often used to refer to the soul.
The Soul Loves, forgives, and understands.

EGO SELF; has free will to grow as it chooses.
Ego has an important role to play, that of keeping you safe and alerting you to danger. Ego is always seeking to find where you fit in, judging or trying to be in control. Ego is all about competition or comparison; right/wrong, win/lose. Ego is the mind`s false identity, based on beliefs. Ego demands; avoids pain; is greedy; is motivated by the external world; resistant to change.
Ego loves to be the VICTIM or the MARTYR.
SHADOW SELF, the dark side, the part that can be negative, doubting, mean, critical, deceiving. Everyone has a shadow self, a hidden self, the side of you that you try to keep hidden, such as old emotions or difficult feelings. Shadow Self loves to hide, out of sight, and is often referred to as the dark side of a person.
Through Self awareness, we learn to recognize and embrace our shadow selves into ourselves.

> *Empowering Moments -*
> *What am I not seeing or willing to*
> *accept about myself? What am I hiding?*

ENERGY IS EVERYTHING – INCLUDING YOU

BE an Observer - Watch and Learn

Observe - Objective
Pay attention to; take notice; be watchful; be present but take NO part in what is happening.
Observation – Soul-driven.
facts collected; facts are the truth.
Neutral, no bias or agenda

Judge – Subjective
Form an opinion or give an opinion; estimate worth; come to a decision.
Bias-based, competition, comparison.
Judgment -is EGO driven.
An opinion; the power of discrimination; faculty of mental perception; criticism.

Be the Observer,
be able to recognize when Ego shows up and you are judging or when Soul shows up and you are LOVING.

Observer or Judge, which are you being?

Take a step back, step out of the equation and observe what is happening to you and around you. It is from this vantage point that you will be able to see the bigger picture and become the Observer of yourself.

OPINIONS

Everyone has FREE WILL to think for themselves. Everyone has an opinion - their own thoughts, perspectives, or beliefs based on their own experiences and knowledge gained up until this present moment.

Their opinion is THEIR OPINION... Full Stop.
Their business is THEIR BUSINESS... Full stop.
That's it, we each have our own, and... it's OK.
It is simply an opinion, a perspective... Full Stop.

Set yourself FREE. Only if you allow other people`s opinions to affect you, will they have any control or influence over you. You do not have to agree, disagree, defend, comment, approve, or disapprove.

Simply say - **Thank you for sharing your opinion.**
When asked if you have an opinion, simply say -
Yes, I have my own opinion, thanks for asking.
Will I share it? No, not always. What I think and feel is my business, it may be similar, it may be different and that's ok. Sometimes it is a matter of accepting each others` opinions without trying to convince one or the other that theirs/yours is more important, right or wrong. **It is simply AN OPINION.**

Only when we get caught up in Ego do we create issues, arguments, or get offended. The EGO always wants to be right, defend itself, or be offensive.

Step out of the drama and Ego and become an observer of yourself as you participate in life.
Be aware of who you are being in this moment.

Who are we?

We are **Eternal Infinite Unlimited Beings**
living a human experience here on this Earth plane.

Spirit is the very essence of life;
the energy that creates all living things; the energy
that resides within us and around us; the energy of the
Universe, Source, GOD, Higher Self, Divinity, Cosmic
Intelligence, Creator of ALL that is.

We are as ONE; Humanity itself.
We are connected; Aspects of the Whole.
We are Spirit; Aliveness and Awareness.
We are Divine Energy; Soul Source Energy

In Spirituality, everything has an equal value.
There is no better/worse, good/bad, **it simply all
exists, and co-exists, together as one,** integrating,
interweaving, fusing, melding, ebbing and flowing,
synchronized, magically as we evolve.
**Spirituality is ... Truth, Connection, Wisdom,
Understanding, and LOVE.**

We discover answers within ourselves when we acknowledge that we are **SOUL, SPIRIT, HUMAN;** when we accept that we are more than our physical bodies; understand we are all energy, vibrations, and frequencies of light, colour, and sound; awaken our conscious awareness and realize how our subconscious and superconscious minds work; allow, accept and embrace all of our emotions; open our hearts to LOVE; make friends with all aspects of ourselves; realize we are all as ONE; when we stop allowing EGO to be in charge; accept life is happening for us, not to us.
Spiritual Enlightenment is an ongoing process.
At each unfolding level of consciousness, the experiences we have also change. As we evolve, we approach each new moment from a different place of awareness, compassion, and understanding.
We become a different version of ourselves each time we learn and grow from our own experiences. We are always creating our current STATE of BEING.
Qualities of enlightenment include unconditional love, a sense of oneness, complete fulfillment, freedom, inner peace, happiness, complete stillness beyond thoughts, bliss, acceptance, and contentment.
We are **CONSCIOUSNESS.**
From consciousness comes **AWARENESS.**
From awareness comes **SELF EMPOWERMENT.**
From self-empowerment comes **EVOLUTION.**
From evolution comes **ENLIGHTENMENT.**
Enlightenment is the Truth of who we are.

We are the **CATALYST of our own life experiences,** we are always in motion, ever-changing, ever-evolving. We are each responsible for our own happiness, as well as our own state of being in any given moment.

ENERGY IS EVERYTHING – INCLUDING YOU

Understand the Laws of the Universe

Spirituality is not about religion or beliefs, it is about your current state of consciousness.
What people choose to believe is their choice. Many religions provide guidance or give comfort and support in times of need but are also based on limiting beliefs.
Spiritual Awareness is about understanding the bigger picture, knowing why we are all here on Earth; awakening to our truth, and evolving.
It is the process by which we begin to explore our existence to become whole again. It is about reconnecting to our Soul and Source; removing the programming/conditioning that has been limiting us or keeping us stuck, and realizing our full potential.
Spirituality is about self-awareness and realization. Within this Earth plane, we are governed and limited by the **LAWS of the UNIVERSE,** we do not have to believe in them, they just EXIST. Some of them are; the laws of Gravity, Magnetism, Resonance, and Truth. There are many many laws to consider when seeking to evolve. I encourage you to research these for yourself as there are too many of them to list here.

Enlightenment is embracing the wholeness of who we are collectively and being aware of that wholeness. It is about accepting all aspects of ourselves including our Ego and our Shadow Self, completely without any judgment or criticism.

It is more than the physical world that we know through our five senses, it includes the invisible world that we sense through our innate SOUL sense - 1st (6th) sense of intuition, inspiration, gut instincts, and inner knowing

We have all come to earth to experience life, and to Evolve. We all choose a life path that will help us have the experiences necessary for our Spiritual growth and to evolve humanity. We are currently living in a time where many people feel lost, alone, or disconnected. Many feel misunderstood, unheard, or invisible. Many are searching externally for what they think is missing. Many are suffering from ailments and are looking for ways to heal themselves. Many are experiencing life unaware that they have the power to help themselves.
**Look no more, for the answers lie within.
Your SOUL knows why you chose this life and what you are to experience to evolve yourself. Your SOUL has your BLUEPRINT, your MAP, your BUCKET LIST. All you need do is to ask your SOUL for guidance, SURRENDER, and TRUST.**

Empowering Moments -
Spend some time every day by yourself, with yourself, focus on your breath, breathe deeply from the belly, slow it down and simply be in the moment... AHH.. Research the Laws of the Universe. E.g., the Law of Resonance, Law of Magnetism, and Spiritual Laws

ENERGY IS EVERYTHING – INCLUDING YOU

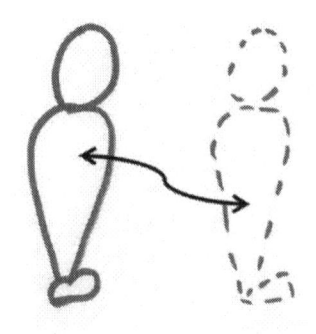

Reconnect with your Soul

**Your CORE SOUL is your connection to the Creative, Source, Universal Energy, or GOD.
All souls are the manifestation of love and light.**

Your SOUL is a fragment of the whole, together we are all fragments of SOURCE experiencing life through human existence. We are all created from the same source; therefore, we are all ONE.
Just like a LAVA LAMP has its Original Source (blob), a portion will break away and have its own little life experience before returning to its Source (original blob). Source always exists, it is in a constant state of change, with no beginning, no end, only motion.
Your SOUL is SOURCE Energy,
therefore it contains the same PURE qualities as Source; Love, peace, kindness, compassion, bliss, joy, happiness, truth, integrity, and pure thought. (Just like a drop of water in the ocean or grain of sand on a beach, contain the same qualities as the whole)
As you deepen your relationship with your Soul, these qualities will emerge and you will begin to function from your Soul's perspective not Ego.

Awakening to the Light of your SOUL is about realizing your connection to Source itself.
Once acknowledged, your Soul will naturally guide you to awaken the deeper spiritual truths within you.
Your Soul is always moving toward greater truth.
Think of the Soul Spark of Light within you, as your Pilot Light, always there to guide you and always ready to be ignited to grow brighter.
SOUL SOURCE; pure consciousness, pure thought, truth, and unconditional love and light.
SOUL ESSENCE – your SOUL SPARK LIGHT within you, that chose to come into existence to experience human form; your superconscious, higher self, your soul identity, and frequency, and the Divine within you.
SOUL PURPOSE - is to experience Physical reality; to experience ALL emotions, master them, and simply, EVOLVE into higher energy vibes of Love and Light.
SOUL LESSONS - the Soul Essence sets up many experiences to master its lessons, it does not limit itself to just one possibility. Everyone has free will and the freedom of choice. Your Soul stays neutral as it guides your Ego and Spirit towards decisions to be made. It is wise to listen to your Soul for guidance so choices can be made from higher frequencies of unconditional love.
GOING WITHIN helps you to realize that you already have exactly what you need, to resolve and dissolve all your challenges, and create everything you could ever desire.
Your Soul knows the truth of why you are here.
Your Soul is your guide, your innermost self.
Your Soul is the very essence of who YOU are.
Allow and trust your soul to guide and lead you.

Soul and Spirit are part of the Creative Force Energy that consists of **pure consciousness.**
It is the very essence of who we are.
Spirit is the energy force, that transfers all the wisdom from your Soul, into your physical consciousness.
Spirit or Energy Body is the energy field of the Aura, surrounding the physical body, it filters all energy in and out of your Physical reality. Similar to how your lungs filter oxygen in and out of your body.
Spirit carries your original energetic blueprint which never changes and is always 100% complete.
Spirit is also the subconscious mind where Ego resides and stores all experiences that happen in physical reality. Every experience leaves a positive or negative imprint on the energy fields. Every thought, emotion, memory, word, or behavior is stored like a photograph. These imprints attract like with like to form a mass or clump of energy, which will then begin to manifest in the physical body. It can take up to 7 years for these energies to start showing up in physical form. Stored emotions like anger, guilt, resentment, and rejection contribute to ill health. Stress depletes energy.

Inge Rosa Knott – " The Theory of Colourtouch"
explains Source (creation), Soul, Spirit, and the Anatomy of the energy systems. Working with Inge has influenced my understanding and the explanations of Source, Soul, and Spirit, that are written in this book.
We are all energy in motion, the more that this energy moves within the Energy Body, the more alive, and healthy a person will feel.

All our belief systems, programming, paradigms, and behaviour patterns are found in the ENERGY BODY or Sub Conscious Mind. Those systems/programs that are not based on LOVE will eventually break down the energy fields, prior to breaking down the physical body.

Everything happens first in the Energy Field, before manifesting in the physical body.

Grounding and Centering are key components to keeping the soul/spirit bodies aligned and connected. A physical accident, action, or a person's thoughts, beliefs, or emotions can shift the two bodies out of balance. Recognize when you are out of alignment.

Mind AND Matter working together = Harmony, Congruency and awareness, of both = Alignment

Mind over Matter =Spirit controlling the physical, creates stress. Mind says Yes - Body says No.

Spirit is learning to meet every experience in the physical realm with compassion and understanding.

Your Spirit Body makes up your PERSONALITY, it has its EGO. It is your current state of being as a result of your choices, reactions, and responses to your own experiences or influences of the outside world.

Your Soul Essence makes up your CHARACTER, the traits you were born with; the foundation of Who you are born to be and help drive your inner desires.

Every experience is an opportunity to evolve.

ENERGY IS EVERYTHING – INCLUDING YOU

Who are We?

**SOURCE is the
CREATOR OF ALL LIFE**

**Pure Consciousness
Pure Love and Light
Infinite, unlimited
Divine intelligence
Pure thought
The truth of what is
Eternal Life Force Energy
Creation itself, Origin.
Highest frequencies**

Creation is a continuous flow of energy, there is always an end and a new beginning taking place.
Similar to the lava lamp, when it creates new blobs as the old blobs dissolve back into the source itself.

The "soul sparks" that are retracted, return to Light, and transformed into new "soul sparks" and a new " life (light) being" is created.

SOURCE - from nothingness, comes - IS-NESS

SOUL ESSENCE (YOU)

For a Soul Essence to manifest in this physical
dimension it must first be created energetically as
Soul and Spirit, each with their purpose.
Each with the same high frequencies of source.
**SOUL is the CREATOR WITHIN YOU,
the INVISIBLE frequencies of you.**
Super Consciousness Mind
Characteristics and Traits determined at birth
Higher Self, True Self, Authentic Self
Inspiration, Intuition, Inner knowing, or 1st sense
Pure Love, Integrity, Honesty.
Your Soul knows your Life Plan and your purpose
for experiencing Life on Earth here and now.
Your Soul Spark is a part of Source,
and is Eternal, Infinite, and Limitless.
It is located within the Heart Centre.
The Light spark within you is your,
lovelight, your pilot light, your guiding light.

SOUL = WHO YOU ARE, AT YOUR CORE

ENERGY IS EVERYTHING – INCLUDING YOU

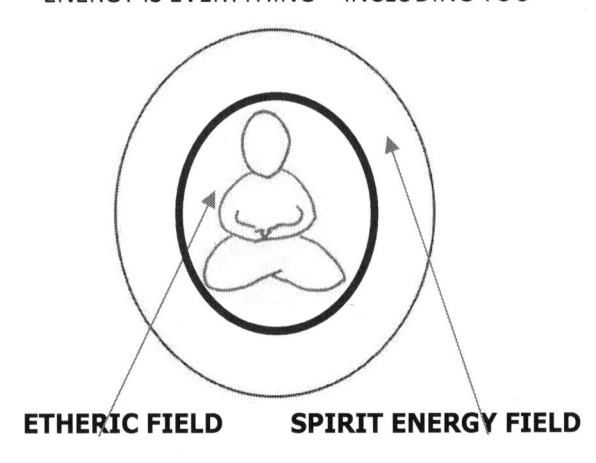

ETHERIC FIELD   SPIRIT ENERGY FIELD

**SPIRIT is the ENERGY of YOU,
the INVISIBLE vibrations of YOU.**

Personality, Passions, Creativity,
Sub Conscious Mind, the Auto Pilot
Beliefs, Programming, Stored Memories
Habits, Patterning, Programming
Emotions, Fears, Judgment, EGO
Mental Intellect, Reasoning
Insight, Understanding, Compassion

The ETHERIC ENERGY FIELD sits just outside the Physical Body and communicates between the physical body and the spirit body energy fields.

It is where the blueprint or map of the physical body is stored. When we work energetically within these fields, we are directly communicating with the physical body itself. Everything is created first in the energy fields before they can manifest in the physical, which means physical ailments can be dissolved back into the energy fields from where they originated.

SPIRIT = WHO YOU ARE, BASED ON EXPERIENCES.

Celebrate - "I AM ME"

HUMAN IS THE PHYSICAL YOU, the VISIBLE TANGIBLE BODY

Conscious Mind Awareness
Conscious Choices, Decisions
Perceived Self, Visible Self
Feelings, Expressions
Words, Actions, Behaviors
The Physical Body itself
Five Senses Awareness
Experiences in the NOW

We can relate Soul, Spirit, and Human to a computer, with the web being consciousness, (SOURCE)
downloaded to the computer (SOUL)
operating systems and programming(SPIRIT)
and the operator (PHYSICAL HUMAN)
We can also relate to upgrading operating systems, once downloaded the OLD SYSTEMS simply do not work anymore. We are continuously upgrading as we discover and understand more about ourselves.

HUMAN = WHO YOU ARE BEING, IN THE MOMENT.

LIFE HERE ON EARTH IS TEMPORARY

We are interdimensional spiritual beings experiencing life in the third dimension, on earth, as human beings. We are here temporarily on this world stage of waking reality yet remain connected through our higher self to many other dimensions of consciousness which we can access through meditation, dreams, or intuition.

As we learn and grow from our experiences, we evolve. If we do not learn or grow, we continue to have similar experiences until we "get it" If we do not "get it" in this lifetime, it means we will reincarnate and come back as other life forms until we do. Reincarnation is the natural process of the evolution of the Soul.

We can be with the same soul family for many lifetimes but switch roles with each other on each visit to earth. Just like a movie star playing various roles in their different movies, for example, Jack Nicolson has played a variety of roles, yet he is still Jack Nicholson. Look at the many roles and movies he has experienced, view these as his many lifetimes of lessons, learning, and growing. He has been the good/bad guy, the funny/serious, paranoid/loving, father/son guy.

Each movie is an opportunity to experience a certain character and role of his choosing. With that same concept, each lifetime, your soul chooses what is needed to learn, then creates a Soul plan.
When a Soul is born in the physical world, there is no memory of this plan and life begins with a blank page. There is no knowledge of what the movie is about, it is something a person discovers with time. This often drives us to find out our purpose in life. We feel something is missing and ask "Who am I? "Why am I here? We sense there is more, but we are not aware of what "that" is until we "become Self-aware" Dreams can sometimes offer insights for us.
PAST LIVES; Exploring our past lives can give us clues as to why we feel an instant connection with someone, or why we are so naturally gifted at something.
Our innermost self knows why we are here and what we have come to discover for ourselves. Our Soul always guides us on our life path through intuition, passions, and ideas that motivate us to follow our hearts' desires, and do whatever brings us JOY.
KARMA; what goes out, comes back to you.
Karma is teaching us to love ourselves; go beyond ego identification and attachments; be conscious about who we are being and how we treat ourselves and others; be responsible and accountable. It is an opportunity to experience both the giver/receiver and the good/bad extremes; get our lessons and EVOLVE.

I always had the feeling that in this lifetime I get it. I used to say" but I do not know what that is..." Now I know without a doubt, "I get it" and I am creating my "free to be me" in this lifetime which will free me from all limitations and old programming.

ENERGY IS EVERYTHING – INCLUDING YOU

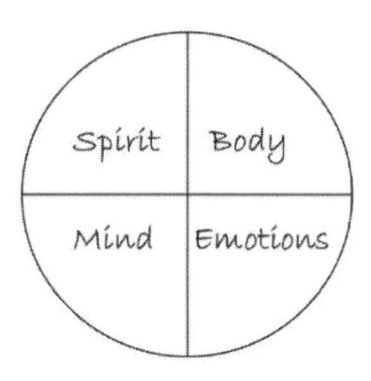

Spirit | Body
Mind | Emotions

Nourish all Aspects of Self

We are more than just our physical bodies, the physical is the visible us, and the rest is invisible.

The four aspects of our Spirit and Body need to be balanced to create good health, wellness, self-healing, peace, joy, and happiness. Just like the four legs on a chair, each one is equally important and depends on the other. If one leg is missing, the chair is off balance and cannot function properly.

**FREE WILL and FREEDOM TO CHOOSE
enables us to EVOLVE or stay the way we are.**
The question is; Are you happy? - YES / NO

THE VISIBLE YOU is 25% of your being

THE BODY - is your physical body and your five senses which enable you to see, hear, smell, taste, and touch the physical world.

Needs - good nutrition, beneficial exercise, adequate rest, fresh air, and water.

THE INVISIBLE YOU is 75% of your being

EMOTIONAL ENERGY FIELD - your feelings that range from Fear and Anger to Love and Joy,

Needs - to give and receive love, forgiveness; compassion, and empathy; to laugh and experience joyful relationships with self and others; to experience and process all emotions freely.

MENTAL ENERGY FIELD - your thoughts, attitudes, beliefs intellect, knowledge, imagination, analytical self, programming, patterning, and habits.

Needs - supportive attitudes, beliefs, positive constructive thoughts or viewpoints, positive self-image. meditation, calming the chitter-chatter by quietening the chaos in the mind.

SPIRIT ENERGY FIELD - your essence and sense of being; your relationship with yourself, your creativity, your life purpose; your relationship with a Higher Power, the Universe, Source, Creator, or GOD. whichever term you choose to use to describe Life force or Life source; connected to all that is.

Needs - peace, calmness, intuition, awareness, openness to your own creativity, inspiration, inner knowing, understanding, and connection to your Heart and Soul, community, and sense of belonging.

When all needs are met, ALL aspects are able to work harmoniously and effortlessly with each other in synchronization to create the healthiest, happiest, and most EMPOWERED VERSION of YOU. It is your choice to be who you are being.

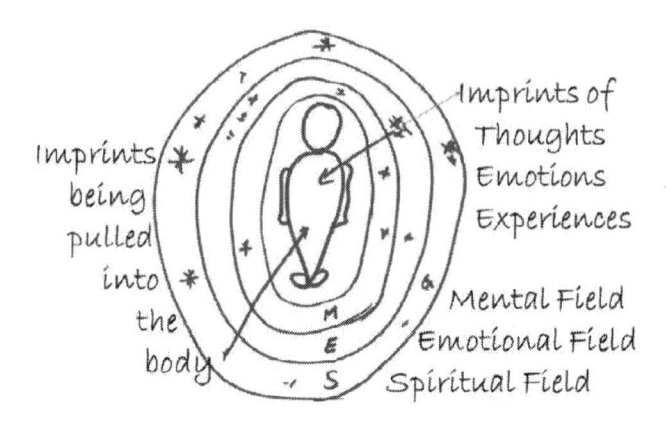

Figure labels: Imprints being pulled into the body; Imprints of Thoughts, Emotions, Experiences; Mental Field; Emotional Field; Spiritual Field

Thoughts and Emotions are actually outside the physical body. They show up invisibly first in the energy fields immediately surrounding the physical body, in our personal space referred to as the Aura before they manifest into the physical body.
The physical body then translates these vibrations and frequencies from the fields into languages of the mind, as words, or language of the body as feelings, actions or sensations.
From the fields of thought and consciousness, ideas or inspirations, are drawn into our minds to be processed.
Our brain, with our memory banks, is the physical processor, it has two parts that work differently. The left side is the Ego mind which is linear thinking, always looking for the logic, facts, or rationale, it thinks in words, the verbal; the voice in the head. The right side is the creative mind driven by ideas, imagination, intuition, nonverbal cues, and visualization, it thinks in images or awareness as the nonverbal way of communicating.

We interpret these thoughts, emotions, and conscious awareness as our own but in fact, they come from a higher source.
Everything originates from Source, which is Thought, Consciousness, and Pure Unconditional Love.
At the physical level, it is only our interpretation of these energies, that we can express or communicate.
Think of consciousness as moisture in the air.
Each thought, emotion, or awareness creates an energy imprint of its own, just like a cloud in the sky is created. These imprints move or linger and gather together, light fluffy thoughts create fluffy clouds, and heavy thoughts create dark heavy clouds.

Just like earth has an orbit of gravitational pull,
the physical body has a magnetic pull that draws thoughts and emotions from the energy fields into the physical awareness and body, to be experienced, processed, and realized. Thoughts, or emotions that are not acknowledged, not expressed, denied, or ignored can become frozen or stuck.

As the energy fields break down, they will begin to break down the physical body.
If we work with our energy fields by dissolving the frozen or stuck emotions, we can restore the energy fields to their pristine conditions, which will then transfer and manifest the physical as a healthy body.

Energy in motion = health and vitality.
Just like the water that flows freely in rivers is healthy compared to water found in ponds, which is stagnant and toxic, it is essential to keep our energy moving and flowing with ease to stay healthy.

MIND MOVIES

Your MIND is PROJECTING your PERCEIVED REALITY into the world that you see, in the same way, a projector is showing a film on a screen. You live your life inside your head and are watching your OWN movie of yourself.

It is your inner consciousness, imagination, thoughts, emotions, beliefs, and feelings all projecting outwards onto a virtual screen that you perceive as your external reality. The screen (perceived reality) is reflecting back to you so that you may see for yourself as an observer, what that looks like consciously. There is nothing outside of you other than the projection and reflection of what is inside of you. It is all perceptions, like a hall of mirrors reflecting many aspects of you, back to you. Each person in the perceived reality you experience; is an aspect of you playing (projecting) out in this external world in the movies you are watching. **Just like dreams** in the subconscious mind where you are the only one who can experience them, the same is true of your waking life, you are the only one who can experience your own conscious perceived reality.

What you perceive as your own reality, is the movie playing in the outside world so that you can be the observer, as the audience of your movie.

Imagine "YOUR LIFE " as "YOUR MOVIE."
Think of all the people involved to create a movie and YOU are the ONE person playing all those roles from the Scriptwriter, Producer, Editor, Director Main character, all the other characters (aspects of self) as well as the audience watching.

YOU are 100% in charge and responsible for everything. You decide what type of movie and who will be in your movie. You could be in several movies at the same time, a western, drama, horror, comedy, fantasy, futuristic, or family movie. Each movie represents an area of your life, work or home, events adventures. Each movie is playing at the same time.

YOU are the CREATOR of YOUR LIFE (MOVIE)
Everything is your choice, your decision, if you are not happy with something you can rewrite the movie, change it, or edit parts out. If you choose to, you can take the movie in a new direction, change locations, change actors, as well as review and edit anytime.

You can create anything in your life (movie) as it is full of limitless potential and infinite possibilities, whatever you desire can be created. **Life is magical.** Excuses for not being able to do something are just false stories that have been created by false beliefs or past experiences. If something is not working out, change it. You never have to get stuck or lose the plot.

> *Empowering Moments -*
> *How is your movie working out?*
> *Are you enjoying it?*
> *What is your perceived reality?*

We each have different Perceptions of the same thing
PERSPECTIVES AND PERCEPTIONS

"If you change the way you look at things, the things you look at change" - Wayne dyer

Everything changes when you look at things from different angles, vantage points, and perspectives.
Perspective; relative importance, comparison.
Perceptions are observations, insights, awareness, understanding.
Perceived Reality is what you have come to believe is true for you based on your own experiences. How you see life can be heavily influenced by others and what they believe. Families, school, peers, religion, and politics all create expectations on how to live life.
Perceived Self- how you perceive yourself is your own doing. It is your interpretation of how you see and feel about yourself based on your own beliefs, experiences, and programming.
Perceived World Reality is the collective outlook of the world stage; the overall view of humanity, which is continually influenced by the media and politics.

Look at everything from a Soul perspective of being neutral, with no preconceived ideas or expectations, no judgments, and no limits, then you will be open to seeing all aspects, all points of view, all possibilities, and all potential. Be willing to listen to others' opinions, be open to suggestions, and to learning new things.

When you approach anything with a limited perspective you will limit yourself. Everything is relative when you compare things, it is only big if there is something smaller to compare it with, it is only dark if there is light, only hot if there is cold. This is the duality and polarity of the contrasting world in which we live.

No two people see or experience the same moment in the same way.

We are all having our own individual, unique, experiences based on our own Life plans.

Everyone has their own way of processing and interpreting an experience, based on their existing knowledge and previous experiences in life.

Everyone has their own thoughts, emotions, opinions, and reacts or responds differently, and that's ok.

Looking at life from a higher level of awareness, from a soul's perspective, that of love, compassion, and understanding, will change every experience dramatically to that of gratitude and wisdom.

Look with fresh eyes from a different viewpoint.

A Soul perspective helps create wisdom within.

> *Empowering Moments*
> *How do YOU perceive YOURSELF?*
> *How do YOU perceive others?*
> *How do you perceive what is happening in life?*

ENERGY IS EVERYTHING – INCLUDING YOU

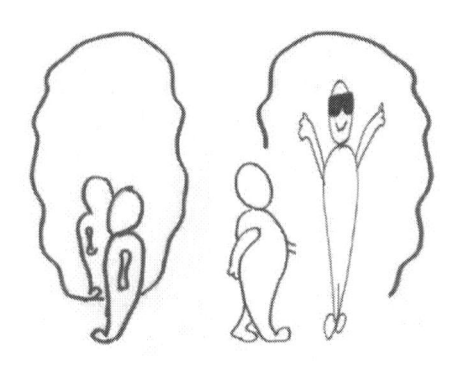

See what life is reflecting to you

**Life is always reflecting back to us
the TRUTH of who we are as humans.**
When we want to learn more about ourselves,
all we need to do is look closely at the people
we interact with each day or look more closely
at the world around us to see what is happening.
Wars, lack of communication, greed, no acceptance,
no tolerance, fear, separation, and division of society.
Conversely, acts of compassion, support, community,
benevolence, acceptance, open hearts, love, and joy.
**We will find many clues that will help us
to see ourselves more clearly.**
It is like living in a world of mirrors reflecting to us.
We learn what to explore within ourselves as our
experiences give us clues about where to start.
We experience what something looks and feels like
firsthand. Sometimes it may be something we can
easily acknowledge that exists within us. Sometimes we
need to look more deeply to see if it is something we
need more of or less of; or something to be grateful for
that we do/do not behave, think or act that way.

All of our experiences can give us immediate feedback about the traits, characteristics, or qualities that we have within us, aspects that may be hidden, aspects that we can embrace or change if we choose to, and aspects we may or may not be aware that they exist.
The Universe is always providing us with clues.
If we are willing to take a closer look at ourselves then we will be able to learn about ourselves more quickly if we become both the participant and the Observer. It is good to start with the people who annoy or frustrate us the most, as they are trying to get our attention and by being right in our faces, they are making this lesson or experience, a priority for us right now. The conflicts that we experience with others is reflecting the conflicts within ourselves.

List the traits that annoy you, then look at those same traits within yourself. They may or not be present, but you will be able to validate that for yourself.
If someone is lying to you or not listening to you, then look at how you are lying or not listening to yourself or your inner guidance. If someone treats you or someone else badly, look at how badly you are treating yourself.
Buddha once said
"All we are is a result of what we have thought"
... oh the power of our thoughts!

> *Empowering Moments*
> *It is so much easier to see traits in others than it is to look directly at ourselves. Be an Observer.*
> *This is a liberating, powerful, skill to learn.*
> *What is life reflecting back to you about you?*
> *What does your outer reality look and feel like?*

ENERGY IS EVERYTHING – INCLUDING YOU

Hello Me

Greet yourself each Morning.

It took me a little while to fully understand or embrace this concept. My own **AHA** moment was realizing that it was indeed the **TRUTH** of how I was treating myself, how I thought about myself, and how I saw myself.

Everything in life is reflected back to me so that I can SEE ASPECTS of MYSELF, for MYSELF.

I was not always willing to accept what was showing up at first but now I am always willing to explore and discover whatever is reflecting back to me.
It demonstrates the frequencies I am surrounded by.
I embrace each experience and every person in life.
I am able to Love and appreciate each of them,
after all, they are me, they are a reflection of what
I am projecting into the world around me.

Self Awareness is key to Self Realization.
Self Realization is key to Self Actualisation
Self Actualisation is Creating your own Reality.
Creating your own Reality is Freedom to be YOU.

The concepts of Mirror Mirror and Mind Movies are essential to grasp and understand. Both are showing you exactly who you are being, who you are becoming, and where you are currently headed, in your life.
**What you do NOW, in this moment,
is creating who you are, in this moment.**
Remember nothing ever stays the same,
you are in a constant change of ebb and flow.

You truly are who/what you think and believe you are.
Be willing to look at your thoughts, words, behaviours, and what you believe to be true for you currently.
Be willing to be honest with yourself, without judging.
Be willing to see both the positive/negative aspects.
Accepting and being at peace with who you are in this moment, is something you must look at for yourself. (R.A.T.S. p114) When you can recognize and acknowledge who you are being, the next step is to check in with your heart and soul and ask yourself,
"Is this my truth, is this aligned with the truth of who I am and who I am born to be. **How does this resonate for me, does this bring me Joy?"**
Only you can answer this. Be aware of what is pulling you out of alignment or what feels out of sync for you.
Be kind to yourself. Always approach introspection with loving energy, compassion, and understanding.
Celebrate all that is wonderful about you.

> ***Empowering Moments***
> *Make a list of the people who irritate you*
> *Look at their characteristics and traits*
> *How are they reflecting back to you?*
> *What are they showing you about yourself?*
> *Are you willing to explore what you discover?*

ENERGY IS EVERYTHING – INCLUDING YOU

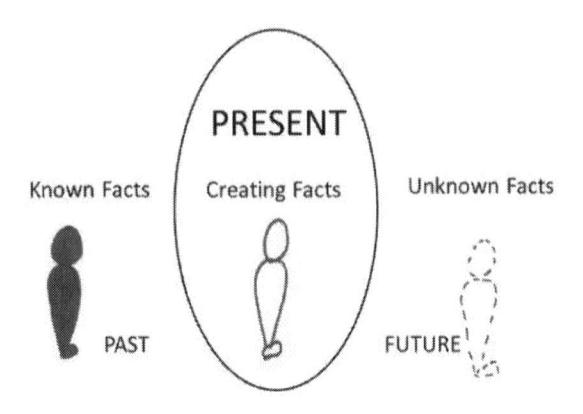

```
          PRESENT
Known Facts   Creating Facts   Unknown Facts

   PAST                         FUTURE
```

Live in the Present

Yesterday is History, Tomorrow is a Mystery
Today is a gift that is why we call it The Present.
NOW, THIS ETERNAL MOMENT, IS ALL WE HAVE
We are past, present, and future, all in one, as one.
We are all able to travel through linear time as we
think about the past, present, and future, but it is
important that we **LIVE** in the **HERE** and **NOW**
and place our focus and awareness on what we are
experiencing in this **MOMENT.**
**This is the MAGIC MOMENT that ignites the
CATALYTIC MOMENT that creates the
MOMENTUM for a MOMENTOUS Life!**

It is **NOW,** this **MOMENT**, that we are able to
make conscious choices for ourselves. These choices
will determine our future experiences, heal our past,
keep us aligned with our true authentic selves and
create our happiness. What we do in this moment,
is evolving into the next now moment, which becomes
this now moment, **the continuous ETERNAL NOW.**

The past is the past, we cannot change what has happened in the past, and what we did or said cannot be unsaid or undone. It has become a fact in history.

What we can do is change how we feel about past events or experiences and we can change how we store the emotions and memories that we have consciously or unconsciously attached to them.

We can choose to let go of painful emotions and memories that are eating away at us. We can learn to forgive and accept so that we can be free of those past hurts, guilt, regrets, anger, or memories, and be free of the connections or ties to the people who caused those painful experiences.

Living in the Present is empowering, it is here and now that we can work with the past and create our future. **This moment has power and potential.**

In the present, we have the opportunity to live each day to the fullest, enjoy each moment, and create wonderful new experiences that will become new memories. It is in this NOW moment that we choose how we wish to respond to whatever is happening, and accept that it is happening for us, not to us.

It is only HERE and NOW that we can help ourselves to understand our past experiences so that we may learn grow, and evolve from them.
It is HERE and NOW that we can accept responsibility for what is and be open to the infinite potential of limitless possibilities. It is HERE and NOW that we are empowered to create our lives with free will.

ENERGY IS EVERYTHING – INCLUDING YOU

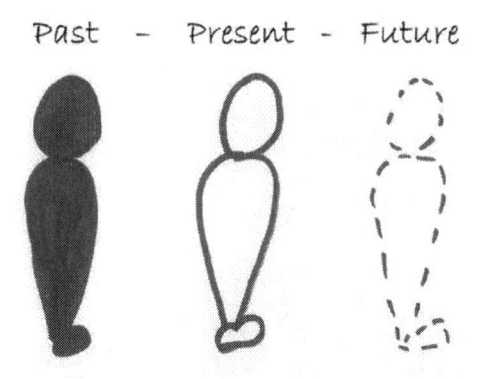

Past - Present - Future

Spend Energy Constructively

We are the total sum of all our experiences that have happened or are about to happen to us. Everybody has to have their own experiences and come to their own conclusions. We cannot tell anyone what to do or how to feel, they must decide that for themselves.

Too much time spent in the past or dreaming about the future is a waste of energy, it takes precious time away from LIVING TODAY, NOW. A person who only talks of their past holiday and planning their next holiday is not present, they are always elsewhere in their minds, escaping or avoiding their own life that exists where they are now.

Each day, begin with phrases like -
"I wonder what wonderful things will happen"
"Today, I am open to receiving miracles"
"I embrace everything today with Love"
"Today is an amazing day of opportunities"
"I am fully present today, in every way"

HAZEL BUTTERWORTH

SOUL WHISPERS

Yesterday is a MEMORY
Yesterday is HISTORY
Yesterday is GONE

Tomorrow is a DREAM
Tomorrow is a MYSTERY
Tomorrow is NOT YET REAL

TODAY we can EXPERIENCE EVERYTHING
TODAY we can RECALL the Past
TODAY we can DREAM of the future

TODAY we have FREE WILL to CHOOSE
TODAY we have POTENTIAL
TODAY we have OPPORTUNITIES

TODAY we are ALIVE
TODAY we are CONSCIOUS
TODAY we are EVOLVING

TODAY is HERE
TODAY is NOW
TODAY is REAL

JUST FOR TODAY
LIVE, EMBRACE, AND ENJOY
EACH AND EVERY MOMENT
and CONSCIOUSLY CREATE
THE LIFE YOU WERE BORN TO LIVE

HB

ENERGY IS EVERYTHING – INCLUDING YOU

I THINK THEREFORE I AM
*"As he thinks, so he is;
as he continues to think, so he remains."*
— ***James Allen, <u>As a Man Thinketh</u>***

First, there is thought, **PURE THOUGHT**
Everything begins with **thoughts**
Thoughts become **actions**
Actions become **habits**
Habits become **character**
Character becomes **traits**

**We are, who we think we are,
at any given time.**
what we think, what we perceive,
what we understand or comprehend, and
what we believe to be true for ourselves,
will all manifest into WHO we are currently being.

> ***Empowering Moments*** -
> *Who/what do you think/believe you are?*
> *Who are you being today?*

Conscious Mind — visible — 10%
Choices, thoughts, perceptions, short term memory

Subconscious Mind — most of which is hidden below the surface — 90%
Autopilot — beliefs, habits, emotions, values, stored knowledge, Long term memories

Unconscious Mind — not visible
instincts

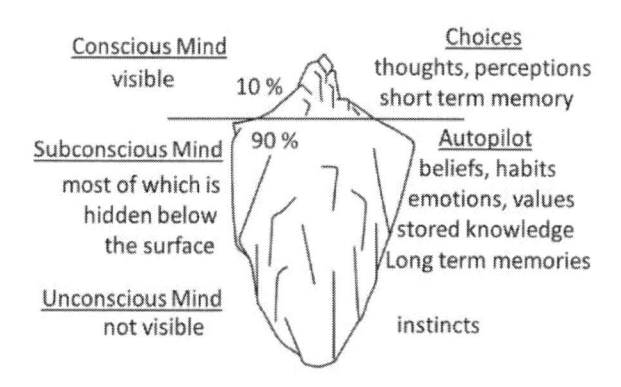

CONSCIOUSNESS AWARENESS

Conscious Mind - the physical mind, our thoughts, decisions, choices, opinions, self-talk, the perceived self of who we think we are and who we are being, and the intellectual self, experienced through the five senses.

Sub Conscious Mind - the automatic mind where our autonomous systems run continuously in the background; all of our body systems that we do not think about; our programming, patterning, habits, beliefs, skills, kinesthetic knowing, stored knowledge, and memories of all our experiences.

Super Conscious Mind - the higher mind, intuition, or true self, intelligence, comprehension, ideas, understanding, knowing the absolute truth of what is, the observer that is detached and understands the soul`s plan and life purpose, the guiding source that keeps us on track and aligned.

Consciousness – the source of ALL thought,
Divine Intelligence, the truth of what is.
Sometimes we need to bring the unconscious to the surface, so we can consciously choose which programming, beliefs, and habits to keep or let go of.

Grow Community

COLLECTIVE CONSCIOUSNESS

Humanity is the average of 7.5 billion Soul sparks. **Collective consciousness** is the result of shared beliefs, ideals, values, attitudes, and morality, in action. It is the extremes existing together within society; the good/bad or Soul guided/Ego driven individuals, who together create a unified field of energy. It is a shared way of thinking and understanding of the world in which we exist; the overall perceptions; and the shared interpretations of life, shaped by personal experiences.

It is what we are all awakened to, and aware of. It is the shared views and outlooks on life that create the connections of like-minded souls to form groups and organizations, thus creating a sense of belonging and community. These shared views help build societies, uniformity, and solidarity. Short-term memory, current views, temporary beliefs, and habits all are part of fads and phases that influence society at any given time. As Self awareness expands, the collective consciousness also expands exponentially.

Collective Unconsciousness is the combination of the unconscious mind that exists in all human beings. *Carl Jung believed that the deepest unconscious mind is genetically inherited and not shaped by personal experiences. The unconscious mind is the driving force of the automatic mind; the underlying programming and patterning that society and generations have enforced on us; anything that no longer requires a conscious thought connection, and we do without thinking.* We continue the same family paradigms.
Being unconscious in a conscious world creates robotic behaviours. We are no longer curious or question the world we live in, we simply follow. We conform to everything; we believe the information we are given without researching it; we accept others' beliefs as our own; we lose our desire to be creative and intuitive; we dampen our enthusiasm and passion. We automatically follow the consensus because of our need to fit in and be accepted in society.

The ENERGETIC EVOLUTION is happening NOW.
We are living in exciting times, we are evolving into a New Earth, a new way of living in PEACE and JOY. It is not about changing what we already have, it is about CREATING a different way of living life; one that is consciously created from the HEART and SOUL, not driven from the EGO mind; one that encourages spirituality; one that supports each other; one that is filled with Love, compassion and understanding; one that is kind and benevolent; one that is intuitive and inspired by our own ideas and insights.
It is about consciously choosing for ourselves and creating a world of abundance for everyone.

ENERGY IS EVERYTHING – INCLUDING YOU

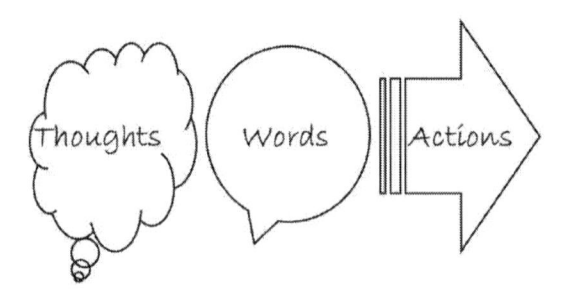

Thoughts → Words → Actions

Be Conscious Aware of these

INSPIRED INTENTIONS

Intention -
An idea, vision, goal, plan, or purpose that you intend to carry out, achieve or accomplish. A clear statement of an outcome you want to experience. A commitment you make to yourself. Intentions guide and influence your activities, thoughts, attitudes, and choices.

Inspired -
Inspiration awakens us to new possibilities and transforms the way we perceive our capabilities. Inspired people are excited about their goals, more creative, flexible, and adaptable.

Inspired intentions -
An intention is driven by passion, desires, or creativity. Inspirations that come from the heart, not the head.

> ***Empowering Moments -***
> *What are some of your intentions/goals?*
> *Are you inspired to achieve them?*
> *What motivates you to commit to them?*
> *What actions can you take today?*

DON`T, NOT, NO

**The vocabulary that we use
constantly shapes our reality.**
The universe takes everything literally as it is spoken,
just like a young child takes everything literally.
Mr. Rogers was very aware of this, he chose his words
very carefully. In one episode talking about taking
blood pressure, he rephrases " blow up the cuff" to
"inflate the cuff". Be aware of your words.
**If I said ... "Don`t think of pink elephant... "
what did you think about? ...** Pink elephant?
We often make statements about things we DO NOT
WANT to invite into our lives, for example
I don`t want the flu; I don`t want a job that's long
hours; I don`t want a partner that is controlling,
however, don`t, not, and no are three words to avoid.
Energy follows thought, which means the thing you do
not want, is the very thing you are thinking of,
visualizing, and inviting into your life, flu, long hrs, or
controlling. The universe does not hear the "Not or NO"
**Rephrase the words to reflect what you DO
WANT to invite into your life. FOCUS ON THE
SOLUTION, NOT THE PROBLEM, FOCUS ON THE
OUTCOMES NOT THE OBSTACLES. " I have a
strong immune system " or "I am healthy"**
Children are a great example, Johnny, no; Johnny
don`t touch, you`ll break it: Johnny don`t do that
you`ll get hurt. Children respond the same way, they
hear what you don`t want and proceed to do it, just
like the pink elephant scenario. Children learn NO, what
"not" to do and limitations from day one.
**It is important for parents to teach and
encourage kids to do what they CAN DO.**

Implement R.A.T.S technique

R.A.T.S. - this is a fabulous easy to remember technique that I created to help students who wanted to make changes in their life but did not know how or where to start.

You cannot make any changes unless you are fully consciously aware of your current thinking, behavior, belief systems, patterning, and programming or what you have currently stored emotionally or mentally in your physical body.

R.A.T.S. helps you to create that self-awareness so that you are able to make those changes possible for yourselves.

**If you are aware, you can do something.
If you are oblivious, you can do nothing.**

First, we must listen and hear what we are speaking and thinking, acknowledge it, then take an action and surrender to success.

R - Recognize - It is important to listen and hear the words you are speaking or thinking; they are clues to help you identify if they are helping or hindering you. You must be able to catch those words if you are to change them.

A - Acknowledge - When you catch a phrase, celebrate, do not judge or criticize, simply become aware that your thoughts or actions are either helping or hindering you, supporting you, or depleting you.

T - Take Action - this is an opportunity to rephrase your statement or to acknowledge it was the "old" you. "This is what I choose to say, think, feel. NOW" Change it instantly, in that moment, to something that does support you. Sometimes action is No action, it's ok as it is, simply breathe, and be one with it.

S - Success, Surrender the outcome, to bring about changes in your life. Let the new words, thoughts, or emotions filter into your awareness and function from this new way of thinking or being. Simply change your operating system, just like an upgrade from Apple or Windows, and start living that way.

It can be as simple as this,
Choose, in this moment to upgrade,
to your NEW operating system,
of what to think, do, say or be.
Just like upgrading your phone system,
you simply start operating as the NEW version.
Once you upgrade, the old systems are no longer accessible, so you learn to work with the new.

From this new perspective of operating, this becomes the renewed version of you.

ENERGY IS EVERYTHING – INCLUDING YOU

I am not worthy
I can't....
I'm not good at..
I never...

CATCH PHRASES

I love to catch phrases.

I catch myself saying a word or repeating a phrase that is out of alignment or contradicts my wishes and desires, or diminishes me. It requires that I listen very carefully to be able to hear the words that I mentally think in my head or speak out loud.

If you can catch the words or phrases you keep repeating that diminish you or oppose you, you can work with them to change them into constructive high vibrational words and phrases that support you.

If you are unaware; or oblivious to them, you have no chance of being able to change anything or to evolve and will always wonder why you are staying stuck.

**Self Awareness is a key factor,
Practice ACTIVE LISTENING
and ACTIVE HEARING
to CATCH your own PHRASES**

For example,
sometimes people use a phrase over and over again -

I can`t believe it rained today
I can`t believe I just won the lottery
I can`t believe I missed the bus again
I can`t believe I was selected for the team

I can`t believe is repeated many times
in both positive and negative ways.

Every time a set of words is repeated it becomes a pattern which then becomes a habit. When things become habits, we no longer have to pay full attention to what we are doing or saying, it will happen automatically. While this can be a great process for some things it is not helpful when we are trying to make changes or understand ourselves more deeply.

What happens when you want to believe in yourself, your ideas, or your talents?

Your programming says "I CAN`T BELIEVE".
If you "CAN`T BELIEVE" how can you ever believe in yourself or anything else?
Change - I can`t to I CAN and BELIEVE IT.

Empowering Moments -
LISTEN and HEAR.
What words/phrases do you keep repeating?
How often are you diminishing yourself?
How many times are you saying, I can`t/never?
How many times do you add a "but"?

ENERGY IS EVERYTHING – INCLUDING YOU

DR. MASARU EMOTO
Hidden Messages in Water

I LOVE YOU · I HATE YOU · IGNORE

Treat everyone and everything with LOVE

HIDDEN MESSAGES IN WATER

Dr. Masaru Emoto - *conducted some amazing scientific studies that show us just how much the energy, frequency, and vibrations of our thoughts, words, and deeds impact the structure of water molecules. It is not the word itself that has the power it's the energy or intention behind the word. The tone of the voice is important, the same words that are spoken lovingly or in anger "feel" very different.*

Try this experiment for yourself using three jars of water. This is extremely important to be aware of, for it gives us a very clear insight into how we, as humans, respond to external influences such as words, sounds, people, and the environment.

Being ignored is worse than bad attention, which supports why people stay in abusive situations. Any attention is better than no attention, both the abuse from others and self-abuse are included here.

Being ignored is like you do not exist and nobody ever wants to feel they are invisible.

These studies began in 1994 with tap water, river water, and lake water. A correlation was discovered between a pristine environment and a city environment. Pristine conditions produced very beautiful crystals, water from lakes, rivers near cities, or tap water could not produce these beautiful crystals.

Observations were done after subjecting the water to the energy, frequency, vibrations, and intentions of words, pictures, playing music, and praying. Beautiful crystals formed when subjected to good words, playing good music, especially classical, or offering pure intentions. Disfigured crystals formed with not-so-nice words, music, or intentions. No two crystals were the same, each had its uniqueness.

When we review the studies of Dr. Emoto, we can understand the effects that energy, frequency, and vibrations have on our bodies.
Our bodies are mostly made of water, including our organs which means that the words we think or speak, the images we see in our mind or physically, the sounds we hear from our inner voices to external sources, are all impacting our own "body of water".

When harsh words are spoken, we feel them within, there is a vibration or resonance that feels horrible inside. We have all experienced this.
When we hear lovely words or sounds; we feel the warmth and comfort of good vibrations within us.

> ***Empowering Moments* –**
> *Pay attention to how you feel when you are being spoken to kindly or harshly by yourself or others.*

ENERGY IS EVERYTHING – INCLUDING YOU

Ho Oponopono
Dr Hew Len

I`m Sorry
Please Forgive Me
Thank You
I Love You

Repeat Affirmations to restore balance

HO OPONOPONO

Dr. Hew Len shares this wonderful technique. There are two stages.

First, *is the immediate sense of peace and relaxation as these phrases are spoken or sung.*
These phrases are the highest vibration phrases.
Second, *is what happens over time.*
Each person has their own needs taken care of as they are directed to what is perfect in life, for themselves. The focus is on oneself.

It is about taking responsibility for anything and everything that you may have done to contribute to a particular situation.

Everything comes into balance as you practice.

It is rooted in the Cosmic Truth that the entire Universe arises through "me". It is true for ALL of us, I am you, you are me. We are as ONE humanity.

Ho oponopono is based on saying four phrases. No one has to believe that this technique will work, they just need to be willing to give it a try and see the results for themselves.

I`m sorry - this apology is an acknowledgment that we are sorry for whatever it is that we have done to contribute to or to create this adverse circumstance that has taken place or is presenting now.

Please forgive me - we are asking for forgiveness with the absolute certainty that it has already been granted. All perceived wrongdoing as a result of our actions, past and present is resolved and dissolved. **Self Forgiveness is extremely liberating.**

Thank You - the moment you take responsibility for an occurrence and seek a way out - you are granted a response. The response may not be as you anticipated or expected. Be open to what transpires.

I Love You - Love is the greatest healing power. the very act of loving thoughts will tune your mind into that frequency with remarkable and immediate results. Simply feel love, think about something you truly love, it could be a memory, a person, or your pet, and you will notice how your body responds. Smile; feel your whole body responding to your smile.

Empowering Moments –
Sit in stillness, repeat the words, I`m sorry, please forgive me, I thank you and I love you. Observe. Think of a situation. Repeat the words, over and over. Think of a person. Repeat the words, over and over. Observe how you FEEL before, during, and after.

ENERGY IS EVERYTHING – INCLUDING YOU

Ultimate Consciousness

↑ Enlightenment 700
Peace 600
Joy 540
Love 500
Reason 400
Acceptance 350
Willingness 310
Neutrality 250
Courage 200

Expanding

Contracting

175 Pride
150 Anger
125 Desire
100 Fear
75 Grief
50 Apathy
30 Guilt
20 Shame ↓

Discover the Map of Consciousness

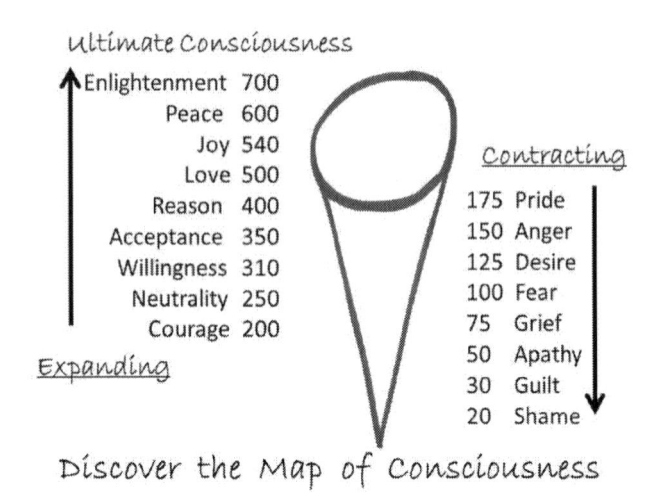

Dr. David Hawkins *wrote a book called* **Power vs Force,** *where he explains that there is a hierarchy of levels in human consciousness. According to Hawkins, people tend to fluctuate up and down the different levels of consciousness at any given time, it is what makes us human. The higher the frequency, the more open we are, the lower the frequency, the more contracted we are.*

Each day we experience many emotions and thoughts, as we navigate life. At the end of each day, we can calculate the average frequency or vibration of what we have experienced during the day. It is not that we never feel anger, it is what we do with the anger that matters. If we hang onto it, it will drag us down, and emotions that are denied, suppressed, or ignored will fester. It is important to allow, embrace and experience all emotions, and to let them flow. Energy in motion is essential for health and vitality.

Consciousness; Awareness of how you are feeling and thinking in this moment of NOW.
Anger, guilt, and resentment, all eat away at you,
they will begin to fester and become toxic,
they are very destructive unless you find a way to
process them or release them. Most of the toxins
in our bodies are expelled by our breathing.
Flush out toxins; As you **inhale, Breathe in LOVE and LIGHT,** as you **exhale, release ALL toxins.**

FEAR and LOVE are the two main emotions that govern us. We are either moving towards Love or away from Love. If you approach everything from a loving perspective, it will influence the dynamics of every experience. **Choose LOVE as your STATE of BEING. Fear is very debilitating, love is expansive.**

> *Empowering Moments*
> *When faced with a fear, ask yourself,*
> *what would that look like from Love?*
> *Let Love guide your actions.*
> *What are you really afraid of?*
> *What is creating this FEAR?*

There are **4 LEVELS OF CONSCIOUSNESS,**
starting with the lowest vibrations.
TO ME = VICTIM MODE, POWERLESS.

BY ME = TAKING RESPONSIBILITY, EMPOWERED.

THROUGH ME = SURRENDERING, ALLOWING.

AS ME = AS ONE, EMBRACING EVERYTHING,
ACCEPTING LIFE IS UNFOLDING FOR US.
LIFE BECOMES EASY FLOW and EFFORTLESS.

ENERGY IS EVERYTHING – INCLUDING YOU

Evaluate The Equation
$A + b = 11 \quad a + 4 = 11$

PARADIGMS

You are the sum of ALL your Experiences.
Every thought, emotion, belief, action, reaction, and all of your experiences, have brought you to where you are in this moment.

Core Paradigm; the underlying deep-rooted beliefs that guide your behaviour; the sum of everything you think and believe that you know to be true.

Your paradigm; is How YOU see the world.
It is the filter that influences how you behave and think NOW, which in turn creates your reality NOW.

Your paradigms dictate everything you will ever experience, without exception. It is based on what you have discovered and come to know as the truth in your life, and will determine your own happiness.

> *Empowering Moments -*
> *What are your core beliefs?*
> *How well are they supporting you?*

You will continue to create your reality from what you currently think and know. If you wish to change, you must first realize that you cannot change anything in your reality if you continue to operate from your existing paradigms and look externally for answers. **If you wish to change your reality, you must create a new understanding,** a new awareness, a new paradigm. Be open to possibilities; be willing to look at new perspectives and perceptions; be willing to take responsibility for yourself; be willing to put effort into that which you wish to create for yourself. Sometimes it is easy to get caught up in false paradigms or to simply switch one set of beliefs for another set without stopping to check in to see if they are the truth of what is or are aligned for you. **The truth is we are all Infinite Limitless Eternal Energy, we are ALL ONE,** we are all currently experiencing this 3D world of duality and the paradigm that we are separate; as once stated by Isaac Newton:
"We are continually trying to evolve to restore our natural state of oneness, yet are continually operating in the forces of duality."

Anything that shows up as a comparison is from this paradigm of separation, hot/cold, good/bad, right/wrong. These are the extreme opposites that enable us to measure variances or degrees of separation. It is important to recognize when you are functioning within these extremes of separation and bring yourself back into a **neutral centre**.
Truth is - it is what it is, no more no less.
To evolve we must recognize and embrace the paradigm that we are all ONE energy in motion.

ENERGY IS EVERYTHING – INCLUDING YOU

A false paradigm is that we all have to be positive all the time or to try to "raise our vibrations when we feel lousy".
This keeps us trapped in the 3D duality world of positive/negative or good/ bad vibrations, judging our emotions and being critical of them.
This approach creates a false reality.

Life is a mixture of everything, when trying to stay positive all the time, emotions that are considered not positive are often denied, ignored, or inhibited.
To be 100% positive, all the time; crushes the ability to experience and express all of the emotions being felt. Emotions that are not expressed, suppressed, denied, or ignored, become trapped in the body creating stress. We are here to experience/understand all emotions.
In truth, they are simply the vibrations of the emotions that we experience. How we feel, how we process, how we interpret, and how we learn from experiencing all emotions is a continuum ebbing and flowing, with no comparison, no judgment, no denying or ignoring. We are simply the average of all our emotions and experiences that we have encountered each and every day, this is an honest reality.

Empowering Moments -
Ask "How does this experience make me FEEL in this moment?" that's it, no good or bad.
Be honest, be true, be aware, allow all emotions, sit with them, be with them, understand them.
"How is this showing up in my body?"
"Where is this showing up in my body?"
"Does it make my heart smile?"
Allow and honor all emotions to flow.

Our purpose is simply to live life joyously.

As we learn and grow from each of our own experiences, we have opportunities to understand ourselves and each other from a place of ...
LOVE, COMPASSION, and UNDERSTANDING.

How you experience your own life will depend entirely on you; how you approach life; how you react or respond to any situation; how you process your emotions, how you interpret the words spoken by others; how much you understand about life; how much you are willing to navigate each and every moment in your life; how much you are willing to release and let go; how much you forgive; and how much you love.

Every moment is an opportunity filled with infinite potential and possibilities.
Every moment is the catalyst for the next moment.
Every moment there are choices or decisions.
Every moment is magical and precious.
Every moment is NOW, this Eternal moment.

You are the creator of your own life so it is important to check in with yourself and question where you are at; where you are going; do your beliefs still ring true for you? Who are you being and becoming?
Nothing is solid, nothing stays the same.
It's all illusions, perceptions, thoughts, emotions, ideas, hopes, etc., concepts that are constantly in motion and ever-changing as we change. It is the awake dream.
Your paradigms (beliefs) are the driving forces that guide your actions that will mold your life.

ENERGY IS EVERYTHING – INCLUDING YOU

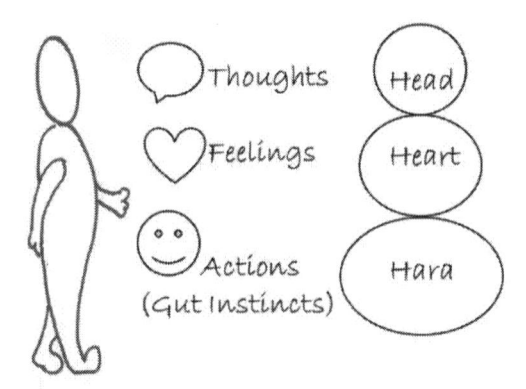

Improve Internal Communications

THREE RESERVOIRS

We have three very important energy centres known as the three reservoirs, the **Head, Heart, and Hara.**
It is important to keep communication open between these centres if you are to make decisions and choices that are in alignment with your "authentic" self, your Life Path, and your Soul Purpose.

When you have thought.   Head
How does that thought make you feel?   Heart
What action will you take?   Hara

Do you pay attention to your intuition?
Do you follow your heart? Do you trust your gut?
Head, Heart Hara, = Inner Guidance and Truth.
The congruency of thoughts and feelings with inner knowing and conscious awareness.

The heart is more powerful than the mind, it emits an electrical field 60 times greater in amplitude than the activity in the brain and an electromagnetic field 5,000 times stronger than that of the brain.
Check out the work of Dr Joe Dispenza and Heartmath.
Live from your heart (soul) not your mind (Ego)

1 Head - THINKING CENTRE, here is where all the busy chitter/chatter conversations take place. We have two minds, the left logical analytical mind, and the right creative, intuitive, inspirational mind. Decisions are often made from the logical analytical mind or EGO mind because this mind can justify rationality.
The right intuitive mind does not always make sense in the present moment, but is always guiding you from the **infinite intelligence of consciousness**.
2 Heart - FEELING CENTRE - here is where your feelings of LOVE or FEAR help guide you. Many people have closed their hearts centres for fear of being hurt. Checking in with the Heart Centre helps you to be aware of all your emotions, it is vital to keep this centre open. It is ok to feel ALL emotions, it is what you do with them that creates issues. It is best to process them rather than hold them prisoners within.
Infuse LOVE into everything you say and do.
3 Hara - ACTION CENTRE - here is where your gut instincts kick in. Sometimes they feel like gentle butterflies dancing or angry bees that create tension. Listen to your gut as it is your GPS kicking in; your gut instincts will guide you to stay on track with your truth. This is your innermost truth detector, that will keep you true to yourself and in alignment with your Soul plan. You always know when something "FEELS OFF" **and be willing to trust your inner knowing.**

Empowering Moments -
Practice connecting to your own Heart and Hara.
Get to know your OWN TRUTH,
what is TRUTH for you, only you?
Know how that FEELS within.

ENERGY IS EVERYTHING – INCLUDING YOU

Learn how to Ground yourself

We often hear the phrase **"Ground Yourself"** but what does that mean and how do we learn to do that for ourselves?

Being grounded is feeling stable,
strong, balanced supported, anchored.

It means being fully conscious, fully present, fully aware of what is happening NOW, in this moment, not here there, and everywhere all at once, scattered, unstable, unbalanced.

It is, being aware that you are connected to your Heart and Soul's inner guidance system, your truth.
It is, being confident, clear, having self-control, able to make good decisions for yourself.
It is, being steadfast yet flexible and balanced.

Your thinking improves, you feel more empowered, you are not easily affected by others or distracted.

Physically it is that feeling of inner strength and power as we stand strong, stable, and tall.
Mentally it is having a strong foundation of knowledge to draw from. Clear thinking
Emotionally is being at peace, calm, and balanced.
Spiritually it is having a good free flow of energy that connects us to the Earth Energy as well as the Universal Energy.

These help to keep you focused, stable, and balanced. A tree with strong roots can bend in the wind, grow tall, and embrace all conditions without falling.

HOW TO GROUND YOURSELF
Place your awareness at your feet, wiggle your toes, and feel the ground beneath you.

Imagine your feet cannot move, they are stuck to the ground. imagine there are roots from your feet just like a tree has roots that reach down into the ground.
Imagine the roots reaching deeper and deeper into the earth until they reach the earth's core.
Feel the power of strength, feel the connection.
Breathe in and out through your feet, or breath in from the top of your head and out through your feet.
Be aware of the strong powerful connection to the earth below you, that helps you to feel steadfast.

> *Empowering Moments -*
> *How does this make you feel, now?*
> Sometimes, you are so much in your headspace that you often feel off-balance or scatterbrained. Ground yourself to restore balance and stability.

ENERGY IS EVERYTHING – INCLUDING YOU

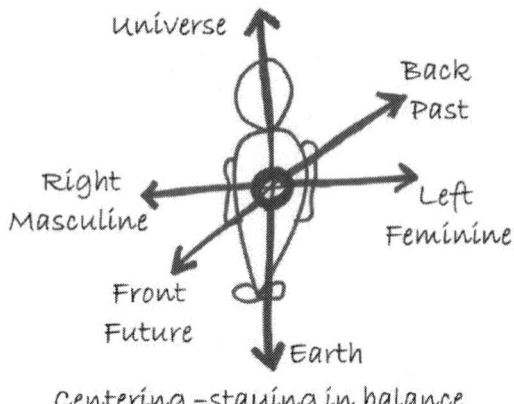

Centering – staying in balance

(Diagram labels: Universe ↑, Back/Past ↗, Right Masculine ←, Left Feminine →, Front/Future ↙, Earth ↓)

**Centering helps you to
find your centre of awareness.**

**It creates a stillness and calmness within,
then brings your focus to a neutral zone,
a place where everything is at peace and ease.**

It is the very core centre of your universe. It establishes a connection with your Soul.

Being centered requires Self Awareness, focus, breathwork, mindfulness, and connectedness,

Being centered creates a state of alertness, it is from here we can make sound clear decisions that are in alignment with our Soul Truth.

The neutral zone, has no agenda, no judgment, no bias, no expectations, it just is.

You are simply breathing and PRESENT.
You are totally IN THIS MOMENT, NOW.

How to Centre Yourself

Start by standing, close your eyes, and be aware of your breath. On each exhale, allow your shoulders to relax, and allow your body to soften.

Place your awareness just in front of you, your toes, knees, stomach, chest, and face, so much so that your weight gently falls onto the balls of your feet.

The space in front of you represents the **FUTURE.** Often, we walk leaning forward in a hurry to get to where we are headed in our future.

Move your awareness to just behind you, your heels, calves, hamstrings, bum, back, and shoulders, so much so that your weight gently shifts onto the heels of your feet.

The space behind you represents the **PAST.**

Often people lean backward as they walk, as though they are wanting to remain in the past. Often some people are more comfortable in their past.

NOW, gently rock back and forth to find the balance point between the past and future, the centre, the neutral zone.

This still point represents the **PRESENT, NOW.**

continued... next page

Move your awareness to the left side of your body, left foot, hip, arm, shoulder, or ear, so much so that your weight gently shifts onto the left foot.

This space represents the **FEMININE** aspect of you, your nurturing, caring, gentle loving you.

Often, we need to spend more time and energy here, to take the time to look after and care for ourselves more and to be kinder to ourselves.

Move your awareness to the right side of your body, your right foot, right leg, hip, shoulder, or ear, so much so that your weight gently shifts onto the right foot

This space represents the **MASCULINE** aspect of you, the assertive, strong, physical go-getter you.

Often, we spend too much time here, driving ourselves fast and furious to achieve our goals and success.

NOW gently rock between the left and right to find the balance point, the still point between Masculine and Feminine.

This neutral zone represents you as **ONE.**

continued... next page

***Move** your awareness now to the base of your spine, imagine it reaches down towards the earth and anchors itself below the earth's surface. so much so that you feel you are a part of the **EARTH ENERGY.**

Move your awareness back to your tailbone then slowly extend upwards along your spine, up to your neck, through your head, and upwards to reach the Universe, so much so that you feel you are out in space and are connected to the **UNIVERSAL ENERGY.**

NOW bring your awareness back into your body. Somewhere within your body, there is a central point where all three axes meet each other, a place of central connection, a place where every aspect, past, future, masculine, feminine, Earth Universe all exist together in harmony, balance, and as one.*

*This is your **CORE CENTRE***

*This is the **CENTRE of YOUR OWN UNIVERSE.***

This is where you are completely neutral.

*This is your **STILL POINT***

From here you can go in any direction, and place your awareness where it is most needed.

ENERGY IS EVERYTHING – INCLUDING YOU

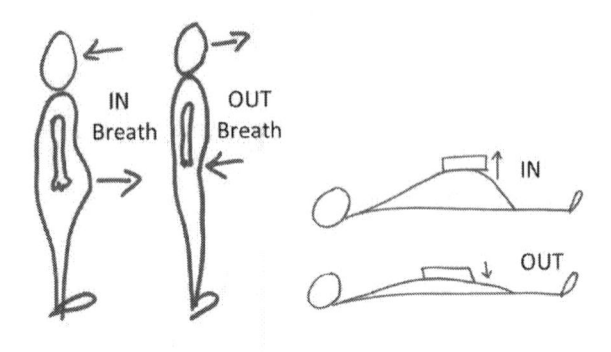

Belly Breathe

EVERY BREATH we take is keeping us alive, but not everyone breathes effectively or efficiently.
Many people shallow breathe, which restricts the amount of oxygen entering the body.
The deeper we breathe, the more oxygen there is present in our blood, which is being supplied to our tissues, organs, and muscles, this results in more energy and vitality.

Slow deep breaths from the belly, help to activate the parasympathetic nervous system, which is where the body has an opportunity to recuperate, regenerate, and heal, and keep our immune system strong and healthy. Slow deep breaths help create presence and stillness, by simply putting all your awareness into your breathing and noticing the sounds and the feelings.

Each inhale = NEW LIFE FORCE ENERGY
Each exhale = RELEASE OLD STALE ENERGY
Breathing is the best way to be present, and in the NOW - PAUSE / BREATHE / BE.........

Our breathing releases up to 70 - 80 % of toxins when we exhale. Contrary to old beliefs, that ladies must keep their tummies tucked in, it is important to allow the belly to expand as we breathe in, then contract as we breathe out keeping the chest and shoulders still. In essence, if we do not breathe deeply, we are not creating an exchange of oxygen and carbon dioxide, leaving us with low oxygen, low energy, and low vitality.

Often panic attacks are created by shallow quick breathing from the upper body.

Clean fresh air and deep breathing is essential for good health and creating PRESENCE.

Place your hands on your tummy. as you breathe in feel the expansion, as you breathe out feel your body relax. To expel more air and toxins, gently push on your tummy at the end of your exhale and squeeze every last drop of air. Pause for a moment, then observe what happens next. After a moment or two, you will be encouraged to take a huge breath in, a large gasp of air, a large gulp of oxygen.

Practice deep slow breathing at every opportunity until it becomes natural for you.

Empowering Moments -
Practice standing up or lying down and placing a book on your tummy to help you exercise those muscles. ***Breathe and be one with your breath,*** *listen to the sounds of your breath as it enters the nostrils and exits the mouth, feel the muscles in your belly and chest as they expand and contract, slow it down, stay with this, experience the calm.*

ENERGY IS EVERYTHING – INCLUDING YOU

Release and Let Go

Often, we are told to just "LET GO"
but what does that mean and how do we do that?

Each day it is important to let go and let flow, any emotions, thoughts, or memories that no longer serve you. Let go of all anything and everything that you no longer wish to store in your physical body. Let the emotions flow out of your body. Keep only those that bring you JOY, HAPPINESS, and PEACE or those you still need to work with to find your lessons and understanding so you can evolve.

You can let go of the attachment to PAIN, GUILT, and RESENTMENT and replace them with LOVE, GRATITUDE, COMPASSION, and FORGIVENESS.

You can create Joy within by letting go of trapped denied, ignored emotions. Breathe in Love and Light, to dissolve any emotion that no longer serves you.
It is important to experience all emotions as they are simply energy in motion, let them arise. Any you wish to release, choose to "Let them flow, to let them go."

Anger, Guilt, and Resentment all eat away at you, they sit and fester, creating toxic destructive chemistry that will continue to eat away at you unless you release or dissolve these emotions.

Repeat this mantra several times a day, especially last thing at night.
I breathe in Love and Light- (deep breath in)
I release all toxins from my body - (breathe out)

THREE DIRECTIONS.
The three directions to release and let go are - me to them, them to me, and me to me.

(take a deep breath and release slowly saying)
I release and let go of anything and everything that
I may have done to hurt or harm **anyone else.**
I forgive, I accept, I release and let go.

(take a deep breath and release slowly saying)
 I release and let go of anything and everything that
anyone else may have done to hurt or harm **me.**
I forgive, I accept, I release and let go.

(Take a deep breath and release slowly saying)
I release and let go of anything and everything that
I may have done to hurt or harm **myself.**
I forgive, I accept, I release and let go.

Now repeat this mantra
I AM Love, I AM filled with Love,
Gratitude, Compassion,
Forgiveness, and Understanding.

ENERGY IS EVERYTHING – INCLUDING YOU

Infuse your life with Reiki

Reiki is one of the most effective ways to create "Empowering Moments" and "Self Awareness" Being PRESENT is the gateway to BEING FREE.

Reiki is all about YOU, your SPIRIT, and your SOUL
Reiki is...
INVITING HAPPINESS into your life
BEING IN CHARGE of your life
CONNECTING to your SOUL
HEALING YOURSELF from the INSIDE OUT
IGNITING your limitless POTENTIAL
COMMUNICATING with your HIGHER SELF
OPENING your HEART to LOVE and to FORGIVE
ACCEPTING, EMBRACING, ALLOWING
CREATING PEACE, BALANCE, and HARMONY
DISCOVERING your TRUE AUTHENTIC SELF
FOLLOWING your LIFE PATH
TRUSTING your INSTINCTS
BEING FREE to BE YOURSELF
Reiki is about embracing every EXPERIENCE, every MOMENT, as an opportunity to EVOLVE.

REI - Universal Life Force Energy – Outside.
Ki - Inner Life Force Energy (CHI, QI) – Inside.
Each Inhale is bringing into the body NEW life force energy (**REI**), to revitalize the inner **KI** (Chi, Qi) the life force energy that is within the physical body.

I AM ONE WITH THE UNIVERSE, ONE ENERGY
I am in the universe, the universe is in me, together we are as one, no separation - as within, so without.

Reiki will take you on a wonderful loving Self Journey to "Remembering Who you are".

Reiki will help you to explore and discover so much about yourself, your life path, your true purpose, your past, future and present YOU.

Reiki is about opening to limitless possibilities and realizing your own limitless potential.

Reiki is about communicating with your inner self, inner child, higher self, intuitive self, aspects of self, multidimensional self, SOUL, and Source.

Reiki is grounding, uplifting, supportive, unlimited.

Reiki helps you to dig deep to uncover the origins of your energy blocks, fears, past programming, unconscious beliefs, and self-sabotage behavior.

Reiki is for everyone who has an open mind and is willing to take responsibility for themselves, it is the best investment you can make in yourself.

Reiki is not something you do, it is an intuitive way of living from your heart, a gentle way to approach everything that life has to offer.

REIKI PRECEPTS, what are they?
A precept is a guiding principle, a rule of thought to embrace, a philosophy of how to live life.
Reiki Precepts are guiding us to live for today,
be present and consciously aware in each moment,
to be EMPOWERED, confident, resilient, and to infuse LOVE into everything we think, say, or do.

The 6 Reiki Precepts are about inviting happiness into our life every day.
By living in the Here and Now, it is impossible to worry about the future or to hold on to any grudges.
They teach us to be present, with presence,
fully aware, awake, and alert.

Just for Today, I am free of ANGER – PEACE
Anger only harms yourself and can create unwanted behaviors. It is important to recognize and acknowledge Anger, look to see what triggered the anger, then find a constructive way to process the emotions and feelings. Even more important is not to hang on to anger or suppress it, holding grudges creates disharmony within you that leads to ill health.

Just for Today, I am free of Worry – SERENITY
Worry does not create solutions, it only robs you of ENERGY. Worry is FEAR-based, it is about what may or may not happen, it creates anxiety, stress, and panic. Energy follows thought, which means the more you worry, the more you focus on the outcomes you least want. Start thinking of what you want to invite as an end result; trust all is ok; all will work out for the good of all. Trust there is a higher power that is overseeing everything. Trust in the Universe and your Soul.

Just for Today, I am Grateful – GRATITUDE
The more we are grateful, the more we will have to be grateful for, and what we focus on we attract more of. Saying thank you for every experience, even those that may be challenging. When you can say thank you to someone who hurt you, that is acceptance of the lessons or growth you received from that experience.

Just for Today, I am Diligent – INTEGRITY
Approach everything you do conscientiously,
do the best you can do with what you have.
Stay focused, pay attention to what you are doing,
be honest, be thorough, be effective, and be engaged.

Just for Today, I am Kind – KINDNESS
Smile, being kind includes being kind to yourself,
you deserve kindness. Be gentle, be supportive,
be understanding, be compassionate.
Often, we can be kind to others but cruel to ourselves.

Just for Today, I go placidly without Praise or blame - LIVING FROM HEART not EGO
Whatever happens, your inner state of Peace should not be altered. Seeking praise or laying blame only feeds Ego and the duality of someone being right or wrong. It is about accepting what is and allowing and embracing whatever is happening in this moment as an experience. Blaming is accusing and judging others, it is an easy deflection and an excuse for a person to feel superior over another person.

Practice repeating these mantras every day until they become natural to you.

Creating the Life of your Dreams.
IF.... you create your reality,
THEN... you can create your BLISS.

> ### *Empowering Moments*
> *What do YOU wish to create for yourself?*
> *What do YOU wish to manifest?*
> *What brings YOU Joy, Peace, Happiness?*
> *How do YOU want your life to turn out?*
> *How do YOU wish to live YOUR life?*
> *What legacy are YOU creating?*
> *How are YOU serving Humanity?*
> *How is YOUR life working so far?*

Dreams, are what you see with your mind's eye
Life is what you see with your awake eyes.
**LIVING YOUR DREAMS - is when
what you see in your MIND`s EYE**
(dreams, imagination, visualization)
**becomes what you see with your AWAKE EYES,
and what you sense with all your senses.**
(the transition from sleep, daydreams, imagination
to an awakened reality of infinite possibilities)

LAW OF ATTRACTION

The effectiveness of LOA is will depend on you.
It is not enough to keep repeating a phrase in the
hopes that eventually you will retrain your mind
to believe it to be true for you.
If you are wishing to be thinner and make a statement
"I am thin", you immediately know that in this moment,
is not true for you, your body knows it's a lie and
creates conflict within you. To say "I will be thin"
always put the outcome into the future and you will
keep striving for the results. When you make
statements that begin with "I want or I will", they
come from a place of lack, that of, I don`t have now.
To be effective, it is essential to make true statements. For example,
"I PREFER" is stating your preference and it is aligned with your truth." I prefer to be thin" is your truth.
To be effective make statements that begin
"I ENJOY...." It already exists, all you need do is
FEEL it and begin living it as your reality NOW.
Align to the frequency and you will experience it.
"I LOVE..." let the universe know what you love
and you will atract more of it.
The second part of attracting is to connect through your heart centre and FEEL what that would be like for you if it was already your reality. Close your eyes, place your awareness in your heart centre and imagine yourself thinner, see how you look, and how it feels, Create from the inside out, from your truth. When you connect to your desires this way, you become a magnet and your outside reality will reflect your inner beliefs. Your desires become reality.

TRIGGERS

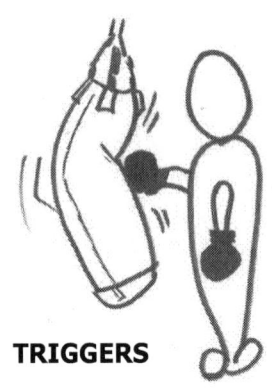

No matter where you are on your journey, triggers may show up, catch you by surprise, catch you unaware, knock you off your balance, and burst your bubble. Triggers may come from your best friends or family. They can come from anywhere, without any warning.
ALL those triggers are messages for you to pay attention, work through them, or discover the wisdom within the experience.
Don't shoot the messenger, on a Soul level, they are here to help you learn, grow, and evolve.
Lovingly "Thank" them (in your mind)
These triggers are giving you clues about what to look at within yourself. Where do they fit in your equation? What was it about the words, or situation that triggered your internal warning signals?
Are those words true for you today? Perhaps it was an old belief statement that no longer rings true for you so when you heard the words, you felt the discord and the alarm bells rang to get your attention.
The triggers are bringing you opportunities for Self Realization and to gain wisdom.

What to do when you are triggered
Often the first reaction is a feeling in your guts, you may feel tension or contraction of muscles, or it may be something feels of. You may feel defensive – that is your EGO wanting to defend you. You may get angry and want to lash out with a verbal attack back.
PAUSE - BREATHE -BE PRESENT-BE AWARE

RATS Recognize/Acknowledge/Take action/Surrender.

Be the Observer and notice what it was that triggered you, make a mental note. Choose a response, it might be you choose to do absolutely nothing in this moment. It might be that you say thanks for sharing your thoughts or that you politely excuse yourself.

When you have an opportunity, sit with this experience for a while and breathe. From a place of awareness reflect on the experience and see what it is presenting, what it is showing you, or what you need to do to evolve at this moment in time.
Meditate or journal with your Soul Self to explore.
It may be a realization; a time to release an old belief, habit, or paradigm; an opportunity to learn something about yourself; create a new paradigm; or realign; or an opportunity to resolve, dissolve and evolve.

Empowering Moments -
What are your triggers?
Who triggers you the most?
When are you triggered the most?
What do you usually do when you are triggered?
How often are you triggered?

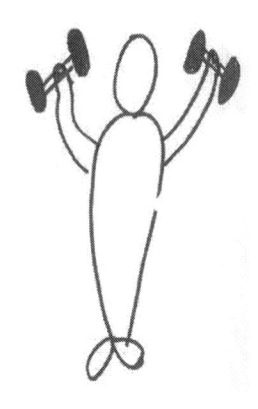

ATTACHMENT and LABELS
What is weighing you down?
What are you holding onto?

Labels can be helpful or harmful, they can make life easier or more difficult. Like with all things, there is the polarity of extremes and a person needs to be aware of how labels are used, especially when labeling themself, as they can become their own beliefs of WHO they are.

Labeling refers to the process of attaching a descriptive word or phrase to someone or something or defining a person or group in a simplified way.
Labels can make it easier to communicate.
Labels can help to organize or categorize for easy find.
Labels can help group similar things/people together.

Labels that demoralize a person can have long-lasting effects, like labeling a child stupid, unworthy, or dumb. Labeling yourself or others can negatively affect self-esteem and self-worth and keep you stuck in a behavioural pattern, or even create self-sabotage.

Labeling someone puts them into a certain category based on looks or what you have heard about them; or judging them before you know even know them. Labeling is a form of typecasting, once given that label, expectations for certain behaviours or beliefs precede any interaction with that person. If someone has been labeled a criminal, the perception is that they are always a criminal until proven otherwise; the expectation is they will always be dishonest or treat people badly because that is WHO they are. This label will create an unwelcome energy of distrust. It is possible to have two conflicting labels, depending on how a person perceives you. It is important to look at how you use labels and the effects they are having. When you place a label on something, you judge and perceive something a certain way, but is it true?

Removing labels that are harmful or no longer true for you, takes self-awareness. It requires you to become the observer and see with a fresh perspective. For example, if labeled at school that you were no good at math, that label can become your belief for the rest of your life, you are afraid to tackle anything that involves math, for you have already been labeled you are no good. Just because someone told you that many years ago, does not mean it is true, not then or now.

***Empowering Moments** -*
What labels do you put on yourself and others?
Which ones are judgemental/limiting? Remove them.
Can you approach every person or experience without a preconceived judgment or limiting label?
Who would you be without all those labels?
(Mom, friend, caregiver, sister, boss, Olympian, etc.)

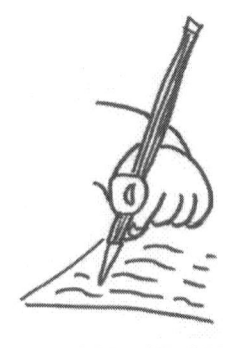

INTROSPECTION

The examination or observation of
one's own mental and emotional state of being.
The examination of thoughts and emotions.

**Introspection is one of the most
insightful ways to learn about yourself.**

Being curious, asking questions, observing,
contemplating, meditating, reflecting, and exploring.
All of these will help you to discover more about
who you are and who you are becoming.

SOUL SEARCHING - Conversations with yourself,
your higher self, inner child, shadow self, or any aspect
of yourself; for example, the victim self, courageous
self, successful self, shy self, past self.
Going within and having these conversations can reveal
so much. Keeping a journal has helped me find the
emotions trapped that have been causing illness in my
physical body. I have explored aspects of me; visited
past experiences; questioned what an experience is
showing me; discovered the root causes or origins of
fears, resentments, and rejection.

For those who are not yet comfortable writing or expressing themselves in a journal here are some tips. A journal is nothing like a diary that you probably kept as a child or teenager. It is not just a record of what you did each day or how you felt.

A journal is....
 - a place to have deep conversations with yourself.
 - an opportunity to express yourself freely without anyone else being involved in the conversation other than you, yourself, your guides, and inner wisdom.
 - can be writing or drawings, or even items you glue into the journal.
 - a special place to keep your inspirations, ideas, intentions, and creative expressions like poetry.

I have several journals, one for poems, one for ideas, one for conversations, and one for aspects of me that show up as characters or past lives I have experienced.

Please note - If you are wanting to do a release and let go, do not write in your journal. Instead use loose sheets of paper, so that you can tear them into shreds as you affirm, "I release and let go of anything attached to this situation; these emotions, or beliefs that no longer serve me"

***Empowering Moments* -**
Create a journal, each morning write for 5 mins,
write whatever comes to mind,
this will help you get started.
Ask questions like What is my priority today?
What message do you have for me?
What do I need to explore today?
Or start with... I am experiencing XXXX,
what is this showing me about myself

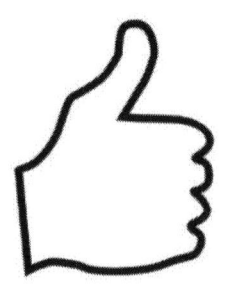

Stop expecting "Perfection" all the time

EXPECTATIONS – believing that something will happen or exist in a certain way.

When we expect things to be a certain way and they are not, we feel disappointed or let down.

When we expect people to behave in a certain way and they don't, it can hurt a relationship as well as you ending up, feeling disheartened.

When we expect certain results and they are not achieved, we feel like a failure.

When we expect to behave perfectly all the time, we put undue pressure on ourselves.

When we expect to do things perfectly, and we don`t, we become critical and judgemental of ourselves.

When we expect to be treated a certain way and we are not, we become despondent.

STOP PUTTING EXPECTATIONS ON EVERYTHING.
STOP LIVING OTHERS` EXPECTATIONS OF YOU.
both are limiting and set you up for anxiety.

EXPECT NOTHING, ACCEPT EVERYTHING.

*"Blessed is he who expects nothing,
for he shall never be disappointed."*
— Alexander Pope

When you can let go of expectations and accept what is, you change the dynamics and energy of the experience and free yourself of limitations. Expectations limit the outcomes of an experience to only one possibility, that which you expect. It does not leave any room for opportunities, possibilities, spontaneity, or the unexpected to show up.
When you can be open to whatever life presents and surrender to the outcomes, life takes on very different energy and Life unfolds itself.

*"When you stop expecting people to be perfect,
you can like them for who they are."*
— Donald Miller

Change "Expectations" for "Acceptance"
I Am who I Am.   They are who they are.
It is what it is. I accept what is.
Expressing your desires or preference for what you would prefer to experience is different from expecting a specific outcome. Be clear on the difference between setting expectations, stating preferences, inspired intentions, and acceptance.

> ***Empowering Moments -***
> *What expectations do you currently have of yourself and others?*
> *What expectations do others put on you, parents, friends, employers?*

YIN YANG

The principle of Yin and Yang is that all things exist as inseparable and contradictory opposites.
The pairs of equal opposites attract and complement each other. Neither one is superior to the other; an increase in one brings a corresponding decrease in the other, and a correct balance between the two poles must be reached to achieve harmony.

This polarity of extremes gives a reference to compare, for example, hot/cold, light/dark, big/small, sun/moon. Just like a coin that has two sides, they co-exist together to make the coin, awareness of both is relevant to the existence of each, to be complete.

Yin is the Feminine, Yang is the Masculine.
Both these energies exist within us. Generally speaking, **Yin** is characterized as inward energy that is feminine, still, nurturing, and negative polarisation, it is represented by the left side of the body, the receiving.
Yang is characterized as outward energy, masculine, hot, bright, and positive or assertive, represented by the right side of the body, the giving out.

To be healthy, one needs to balance the yin and yang forces within one's own body. Giving / Receiving.

BALANCING YIN/YANG -What does that mean?
Some refer to yin and yang as the
light (SOUL SELF) or dark (SHADOW SELF)
Who we are on the inside and who we show up as on the outside can vary, sometimes they are aligned, and sometimes they can conflict with each other. Awareness of who we are being in any given moment is essential to balance these two energies. There are occasions when we need to be assertive, strong-minded, and dynamic, and other times we need a softer more gentle, loving approach.
There are times to give and times to receive graciously. When people say "you must be positive all the time." This is unhealthy. **What you must be, is honest with yourself,** honest with your emotions, honest with your thoughts, and able to recognize when you are being positive or negative. Negativity is not a bad thing. It just means you are having a negative response to something, or are being negative about something. Society has taught us that to be negative is wrong, which is not true.
You were born with FREE WILL, which means you get to choose how much you invest in each of these energies. It is not a case of either-or, which is polarity itself, it is about being aware of your own energy and realizing they both exist within you and you will fluctuate between them. You cannot be both at the same time. Polarisation of one or the other extremes.

> ***Empowering Moments** -*
> *When do you need to be assertive?*
> *When do you need to be gentle and loving?*
> *Be an observer and become aware of yourself.*

```
         WOOD    FIRE

    WATER         EARTH

           METAL
```

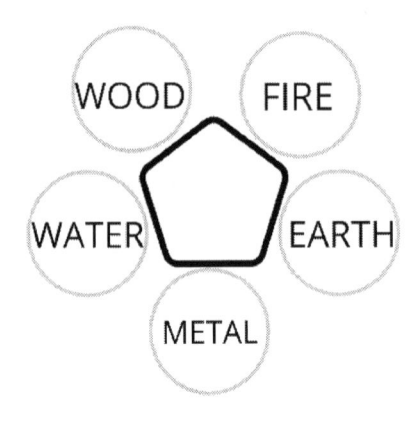

Chinese Medicine - believes that the five elements, outline the relationship between the different elements in nature and the life force energy, or "qi," that flows through them. The basic elements are wood, fire, earth, metal, and water. Each individual is a blend of these elements, and to be truly healthy, they need to be balanced.

Each element also has an association with the body, emotions, seasons, and the five physical senses.

```
FIRE   - JOY. LOVE, HATE         –heart     LAUGHING
EARTH  - EMPATHY, SYMPATHY.      – spleen    SINGING
METAL  - GRIEF, GUILT, REGRET    – lungs     CRYING
WATER  - FEAR, ANXIETY           – kidneys   GROANING
WOOD   - ANGER                   – liver     SHOUTING
```

In Kinesiology and Tibetan Energy muscle testing is used to check that the energy pathways are flowing, as well as flowing in the right direction. A body that is not in truth will test weak. A body that has energy flowing is a healthy body and tests strong.

Fire 火 — Wood 木 — Earth 土 — Metal 金 — Water 水

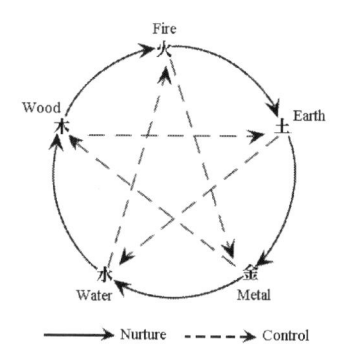

→ Nurture   ---→ Control

I studied Kinesiology, Tibetan Energy (with the five Tibetan rites), and Brain Gym for a while, it taught me about the energy body, the pathways, meridians, and how they communicate with each other. I learned how our beliefs can weaken our energy flows; how our bodies respond to truth; how to make statements that are aligned with our truth; how to explore layer after layer within our energy fields to find the emotion that is causing congestion; how to dissolve trapped energy by understanding the root cause.

It does not matter which school of thought you choose the goal is to understand we are all energy in motion and your body knows your truth. It is essential to learn how to tune into your own energy and be able to read, for yourself, what you are experiencing energetically.

It is essential to keep your energy "flowing".
Think of a river flowing off the mountains, the water is crystal clear, as it slows down it becomes less clear. A pond with no flow of water becomes stagnant and toxic. Your energy responds the same way, when it is flowing its healthy, when it stops flowing, it becomes toxic.

ENERGY IS EVERYTHING – INCLUDING YOU

1, 2, 3.

NUMEROLOGY – What's in your Equation?

Numbers are significant in life but how do they influence you and what do they represent?
Pythagoras believed the world was the amalgamation of the energetic vibrations of numbers. He spoke in terms of cycles, patterns, and waves of energy.
He created a system of numerical interconnectivity and corresponded letters, colours, and virtues with numbers. These numbers are used for metaphysical insights to understand your personality traits, Life purpose, or to receive messages from your guides.

Before you were born, you already had your unique Soul Frequency which stays the same all through your life. This is your Core Soul Frequency.
Birthdate – these numbers have a great significance; they represent the characteristics you were born with. For example, your star sign has its unique character traits as does your birth date. Astrology is one way to discover the life path you chose.
Dan Millman, the author of the book *"The Way of the Peaceful Warrior"*, also wrote a book called *"The Life you were born to Live"*. It is a brilliant reference book.

Life Purpose - In this book, he shows you how to determine your life purpose using the numbers of your birthdate. The energies of the numbers all contribute to the essence of who you are. Birth numbers reveal issues, challenges, and potential for your life path. Each number can manifest in positive (constructive) or negative (destructive) energy.

Your Soul knows why you are here in this lifetime and what you have to accomplish, which is why you may have the feeling that something is missing and find yourself searching for answers. The questions of Who am I, why am I here, are often asked.

This curiosity drives and shapes your careers and relationships as well as influence your decisions and direction in life. This is your intuition guiding you.

Personal year – replacing your birth year with the current year, you can determine what year cycle you are in. Life continues in cycles of 1-9 years.

1 represents new beginnings, 9 endings, or completion.

Birth Name – Each letter of your name has its frequency and vibration. Your birth name is the combination of these energies. Each time you change your name you change your energy, which is why some people prefer to always use their birth name and others deliberately create new names for themselves. Sometimes individuals prefer to be called by their middle name or choose a completely different name because the one they were given did not feel right.

In Colour Therapy each number corresponds with a colour, so it is possible to discover the colours of the vibrations of your birthdate, name, star sign, personality, and Soul.

ENERGY IS EVERYTHING – INCLUDING YOU

Trust your Intuition

NUMBERS AS MESSAGES

You may have become aware of certain numbers showing up repeatedly, for example, 11:11, 222, 555.

You may have noticed a number, it could be a car number plate that gets your attention, or a random number suddenly making its presence known to you. You can even choose a random number for yourself. All these numbers have resonance and meaning.

I love numbers, it may be the time on the clock when I get up for a pee break in the night; or a random number that gets my attention. I know these are all messages for me and my Soul is bringing my awareness to these numbers for me to explore them for myself. There is no Ego attached to these insights.

A great website that I refer to is *Joanna Sacred scribes*. *http://sacredscribesangelnumbers.blogspot.com/*

You can look up any number to find the energy and meaning associated with it.

DREAMS AS MESSAGES

When we sleep, our consciousness leaves the physical realm and travels within the interdimensional realms to receive higher teachings. Our dreams bring awareness, insights, or guidance on how to navigate our daily lives. Sometimes, we receive glimpses of what is possible for us by receiving insights, ideas, and inspiration.
We often dream in stories which makes them easier to understand, but sometimes dreams are very disjointed or scary, these we remember more easily because of it. ALL dreams our about ourselves, even if the characters are people we know. Ask your higher self to remember your dreams upon awakening. Keep a dream journal.

What are dreams showing us?

The truth of who we are, infinite energy beings.
Clues to interpret for ourselves, about ourselves.
Conversations and visits with our higher self, guides, or past loved ones. Opportunities to work with the subconscious and superconscious minds.

To interpret dreams, make a list of 3-5 things, then journal and ask for the deeper meanings. A great reference book is *The Dream Book by Betty Bethard.*

SOUL WHISPERS

**It's a dream life,
live your dreams**

*When we are asleep,
we dream
It appears real in every sense
We see with our mind's eye
eyes closed*

*When we are awake
We "DAY" dream
It appears real in every sense
we see with our physical eyes
eyes open*

*Eyes shut, Eyes open
ALL are dreams,
ALL are illusions,*

*Life is a DREAMWORLD
filled with illusions.*

*When we die
we no longer dream, and
we no longer experience the illusions*

HB

SOUL WHISPERS

It Matters

It matters what you do.
It matters how you treat people,
It matters that you love,
It matters that you forgive,
It matters that you release, let go, let flow.
It matters that you open your heart,
It matters that you laugh, have fun, sing and dance.
It matters

IT MATTERS

YOU MATTER

what you do
and who you are
MATTERS

ENERGY IS EVERYTHING – INCLUDING YOU

Who are We?

WE ARE INTERDIMENSIONAL BEINGS

We are multi-dimensional by nature.
The first dimension is the mineral world and water.
2D is the plant kingdom, lower animal kingdom, and elementals such as fairies, gnomes, elves, and pixies.
3D -We are Spirit beings, with a visible human body, experiencing life in this 3-dimensional earth plane of existence, which is defined by time and space.
We experience the 3D world through our five senses and the interdimensional world through our 1st intrinsic sense which most refer to, as our 6th sense.
There are many other dimensions that we already experience. Through dreams and meditation, we can experience the timelessness of higher consciousness in the **4D** world, we are limitless, we can do anything; we can feel like we are flying in the astral realms.
5D Unity consciousness is where we experience love, unconditional love. It is where the coherence of heart and mind reside, we are no longer caught in the EGO dualistic dimension of polarization or separation. Life is no longer a battle; we are FREE to create NEW ways of thinking/being/doing, through a unified field of energy.

6D- Crystal consciousness is when a person surrenders to the flow of spirit`s evolution. This is the Easy Flow Living that is created when there is no resistance, only acceptance that life is unfolding perfectly for us and that we are all one. We are still able to maintain our uniqueness within these realms of higher awareness
7D is what some refer to as Christ consciousness, is where there is full awareness of the nature of being. Souls take on the roles of teachers or mentors as they fulfill their mission of helping other souls to embrace themselves with expanded awareness and deeper understanding. 7D souls hold the energy and the light for humanity, as we, all together, create a NEW Earth. ***Delores Cannon*** *refers to these souls as the "way-showers" who have volunteered to help with the evolution of humanity until" they get it" for themselves.*

8-11 are higher dimensions that lead from Archetypal through Cosmic to Galactic consciousness and finally **12D** - is the FULL Universal level of consciousness, which is the frequency, and vibration of SOURCE itself.

What we are currently experiencing is a mixture of 3D to 7D frequencies of conscious awareness.
This is the awakening process, awakening to the truth that we are more than our physical bodies, we are all energy vibrating on many frequencies. Ego is low vibrations of 3D awareness. We are evolving beyond Ego, beyond the materialistic way of living with greed and control over others, into a more dynamic loving world of Unity consciousness.
This is the New Earth, the new way of living life in Easy Flow - Awake, Alert, Aware, Alive.

ENERGY IS EVERYTHING – INCLUDING YOU

Believe – Anything is Possible

SCIENCE IS CATCHING UP

Science is able to validate what intuitive and energy workers have known for eons but had no physical ways to prove their inner knowing. Seeing is believing for many, and unless there is something tangible to prove a theory, then it is often considered just a theory with no proof.

Science can now measure **Electromagnetic energy**; photographs can be taken of energy fields around the body with **Kirlian photography**; **Biofeedback** computers can read the frequencies and vibrations within the organs of the body; **Quantum physics** can now prove that even the smallest of particles is energy blinking in and out of existence, that absolutely nothing is solid, it is just vibrating so slowly that it appears to be solid; **Heart math** can measure resonance and prove the heart has far more powerful energy than the mind; **Epigenetics,** can show how environmental influences affect gene behaviour. **Metaphysics**- can explain nature and its reality; the relationship between mind and matter, **Ontology** – is the science of being.

Science is not finite. It is living knowledge that is continually learning and growing in its understanding as it evolves, just like us. Everything exists as energy before it manifests physically. Ideas, inspirations, curiosity, and desires all exist before a person can create a machine or some way of physically proving it. **For the folks who love science,** here are some people who are diligently doing the research, studies, and work to prove who we are, why we are here, how we are part of the universe; how energy is everything, how biology of belief works, how thoughts are energy, how light colour and sound are the medicines of the future along with energetically thinking. Scientists are always making discoveries that help us understand more about how our universe works.

Thank you each and every one of you for your studies.

Dr. Joe Dispenza	Neuroscience; Epigenetics. The Placebo, Becoming Supernatural, Breaking the Habit of Being Yourself
Gregg Braden	Bridging Science and Spirituality The Divine Matrix. Fractal Time, Human Design. plus many more.
Dr. David Hawkins	Map of consciousness; Power vs force
Dr. Emoto	Science of Water & Consciousness
Stephen Hawking	Nature of the Universe; relativity.
Darius Dinshah	Science of Colour therapy
Bruce Lipton, Ph.D.	Biology of belief; Epigenetics
Dr. Hew Len	100% responsible for your reality.
Dr. Edward Bach	Flower remedies
Joyce Whiteley, PhD.	Cell Level healing.
Jonathon Goldman	Sound Harmonics

ENERGY IS EVERYTHING – INCLUDING YOU

SOUL WHISPERS

EPIC AWAKENINGS

Self Awareness, Self Realization,
Self Empowerment, Self Mastery
= CONSCIOUS AWAKENINGS

To AWAKEN is to BE AWARE
To be CONSCIOUS AWARE is to BE PRESENT

Presence; consciously living
awake, alert, and aware
in the present moment.

Consciously creating a world of
Truth, Love, Peace, Freedom
Kindness, Benevolence,
and JOY.

BE A PART OF THE ENERGETIC EVOLUTION

Embrace Life with

Enthusiasm and Excitement,

and ENJOY living each and every moment.

HAZEL BUTTERWORTH

Explore and Discover

PART THREE

If I am the one creating my life,
what must I realize, what must I be?

BE aware of your State of Being.
BE CURIOUS.

SOUL WHISPERS

REALIZE YOUR OWN POTENTIAL

Everyday VISUALIZE
Everyday TRUST
Everyday ALLOW

Every moment is a gift
Every moment is precious
Every moment counts

Be open to possibilities
Be free of fear
Be true to yourself

All in good time
All synchronized
All in good faith

For it is written in the stars
Written in your heart
Written in your Soul

At the end of the day
Let go of any ill feelings and any ill thoughts
Liberate yourself and set yourself FREE.

Step into your Sovereignty
and be in charge of your own life.

SOUL KINETICS –
the dynamics of SOUL, SPIRIT, HUMAN.
Everything is Energy including YOU.
YOU are always experiencing your own "state of being"
which continues to change as it vibrates
on the different frequencies of consciousness.

> *Empowering Moments*
> *Ask yourself these questions.*
> *WHO you are being? Who you are becoming?*
> *What is your current State of being?*
> *If nothing changes, you are on a trajectory*
> *to continue being the person you are being.*
> *Are you happy being who you are being?*
> *Does your life bring you JOY?*
> *Do you wish to continue with more of the same?*
> *If you answered yes, then keep going.*
> *If you answered no, then something must change.*

Even though we are complex beings, life does not have to be complicated, yet most of us have been making life very complicated for ourselves by being caught in the drama of the Ego mind and stuck in old habits, programming, paradigms, beliefs, and behaviours.
Life can be EASY FLOW LIVING,
Life can become EFFORTLESS, when we accept and surrender to nonresistance.
Synchronicity then allows everything to fall into place, through Divine intelligence, and with Divine timing.
Life is a dance of experiences, all weaving themselves into the very fabric of who you are, who you are being, and who you are becoming. It is your choice what you create with that fabric of YOU.
Enjoy creating YOU.

SOUL WHISPERS

BE LOVE,

I AM LOVE

No there, no where
Only **HERE**

No ifs, No buts
Only **IS**

No then, No when
Only **NOW**

No life, No death
Only **EXPERIENCE**

No them, No us
Only **ME**

No good, No bad
Only **LOVE**

Here is NOW
Experiencing ME
as LOVE

BE LOVE, BE LOVING.

Being LOVE infuses LOVE into everything.
Begin by loving yourself first and foremost.
Fill your own reservoir and let it overflow.
Love is both the question and the answer.
Love is the glue that holds everything together.
Love is the chemistry and the catalyst for change.
LOVE IS LIFE - LIFE IS LOVE
BE loving, give and receive love at every opportunity.
Live in a world of LOVE, especially Self LOVE,
Express love for everything, nature, life, and humanity.
AS within, so without... so Start LOVING
Stop trying to change others, stop judging.
Stop trying to change the outside world. Remember the frequency you vibrate with,
is who you are being, the more you are LOVE,
the more LOVE you will experience in your life.

Empowering Moments - Explore LOVE
What does that look and feel like for you?
Can you really love someone if they hurt you?
How many ways can you express love?
What do you LOVE to do?
What do you love about yourself?
What do you love about life?

Forgiveness is love for yourself and others.
To Love is to recognize yourself in others.
Love is the power, Love is the source
Without Love, there is only emptiness

"Love is the energy of life."
Robert Browning

BE A KID FOR THE DAY

Babies and young kids are amazing, they really do know how to live in the present moment. Life is simple, they only do what they enjoy doing and as soon as it no longer brings joy or excitement, they stop doing it. Kids are high vibes, they are so full of life and vitality. **Kids see everything through the lens of curiosity,** constantly exploring and discovering something new. Everything is magical, every day is a new day, every experience is an adventure, every moment is lived with presence, and every emotion is honestly expressed. **Kids see life through the lens of simplicity.**
Kids either like something or they don't; their world is simplistic; they love to play, have fun, and be creative; their imagination is limitless, as they know no limits. There is excitement, enthusiasm, and anticipation, as well as a sense of wonderment for what life has to offer. There is an innocence about them, they trust until such time a trust is broken; they believe until such time they discover it was an illusion, they love unconditionally until they are taught, conditional love.

Kids make great lie detectors.
Kids know love and truth; they feel the vibes and can easily tell when you are not being truthful with them. Parents will try to hide their own emotions and say they are fine when inside they feel turmoil. Kids will instinctively know what they are seeing and hearing is not the truth because of how they feel.

Kids are like a barometer; they sense the vibes.
Kids today are more sensory aware and empathic. They are born with memories of previous lives and have an awareness of why they are here. Because they have such empathy, they are struggling with their own feelings. As kids, they have not yet learned that what they are feeling may belong to another person and that they can switch off those feelings. It is a gift to be able to read the vibrations of others but can be challenging if a child does not know how to process those feelings.

Every day, learn, grow, evolve, then REPEAT.
We can learn a lot from children if we take a leaf out of their books and live simplistically, honestly, with an open heart, an open mind, a sense of play, curiosity, a sense of adventure, anticipation, excitement, and an enthusiasm for living in the moment. Being open to whatever life presents, trusting that it is all unfolding for you, will help you evolve and emerge as a newer version of you, just like the butterfly emerges, a flower blossoms or a snake sheds its skin.

Choose which lens you view your life through and enjoy the "movie" of YOUR life.

Empowering Moments -
I wonder what I will experience today
I wonder what amazing opportunities will present.
I am excited about today.

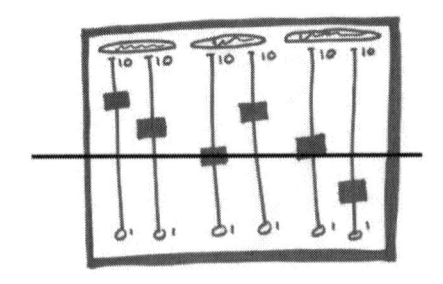

Find your Neutrality

BE IN CHARGE OF YOUR OWN ENERGIES

Everything is temporary, nothing stays the same. YOU are in a constant flux of ever-changing vibrations as you move from one emotion to another, one thought to another, and one belief to another.
This constant flux at the end of the day creates an average that gives you your overall vibration for that day, which you then translate into whether you have had a good day or not.

You have the power, you are responsible.
Your own vibrations will depend on how you respond to each experience and whether you stay in low vibes or recalibrate yourself to restore balance and harmony.
It is essential to be aware of how you are feeling in any given moment so that you can easily recognize if you are being pulled out of alignment, away from love, JOY Peace, harmony, or balance, and into the vibes of Ego.
Remember, we are here to experience all emotions.
There is no right or wrong, it simply is what it is.

Reaction = Ego driven.
Response = Soul guided.

BE AT PEACE

"We can never obtain peace in the outer world until we make peace with ourselves." –
Dalai Lama XIV

Up until now, we have had it backward,
we have allowed the outside world to rule us
when in truth it is we who created the outside world.

Being at PEACE within yourself
creates peace in your own physical reality,
which creates world peace in the outside global world.

BEGIN WITHIN, with YOUR INNER WORLD
Be at peace with your decisions, your life,
your relationships, your past experiences.
Be at peace with the present moment, just as it is.

Empowering Moments -
Are you "at Peace" with yourself and your life?
Regrets, guilts, disappointments, resentments,
anger, and fears, all diminish your inner peace
if you hold onto them or let them fester within you.
Can you let go, resolve or dissolve those vibrations?

INNER WORLD / OUTSIDE WORLD

What if...
The outside world is the illusion
The physical world is your perceived reality
The inner world is you.

What if
The outside world is the reflection of
The physical world of who you are being
that arises from
The inner world, you are projecting.

What if
The outside world is giving you clues
The physical world is the processor
The inner world is where true empowerment is.

What if
you begin with our inner world
Knowing we will create your own realities
What would the outer world look like?

What if
the outside world is the wanting
the physical world is the doing
the inside world is the being.

You being YOU is YOUR purpose
You being YOU creates YOUR physical reality
You being YOU creates YOUR outside world.

BE THE CREATOR OF YOUR WORLD

Earlier in the book we talked about you being the
creator of your own world, your own physical reality,
and that the outside world is merely a reflection
of what you are projecting into the world,
from your own inner state of being.

Creating HEAVEN on EARTH
HERE and NOW

Eckhart Tolle and Anita Moorjani both speak of
creating a New Heaven and a New Earth,
Anita Moorjani speaks of her near-death experience
where she got to experience the realms beyond
the physical and teaches that
Heaven is not a place, it is a state of being.

Eckhart Tolle refers to heaven, not as a location
but as the inner realm of consciousness.
"A New Heaven" is the emergence
of a transformed state of human consciousness, and
"a New Earth" is its reflection in the physical realm.
**"Every human being emanates an energy field
that corresponds to his or her inner state"**

This is the ENERGETIC EVOLUTION

We have an opportunity to create our own
Heaven on Earth, here and now.

We can create our own BLISS.
We can live in Peace and JOY

We can live our "Happy ever after"
starting right NOW, by consciously creating
our own" inner state" of being.

ENERGY IS EVERYTHING – INCLUDING YOU

Grow Community

BE KIND, BE HUMANE

7.5 billion souls all contribute to humanity.
What are you infusing into the world?
How are you supporting humanity?
How are you serving humanity?
What is your legacy?
WHO are YOU?

Ultimately, we are all collectively creating the outside world in which we reside.
This collective dream state or illusion of our perceived reality is the average of the accumulation of everyone's thoughts, beliefs, emotions, and actions, all woven together as the fabric of life, and the global world we refer to as humanity. The world is "of your making."

Everything is Energy, including you
It is essential to be able to understand that you are simply energy in motion, ever-changing, ever-evolving, and ever-emerging into newer versions of yourself.
It's your life, how you live it, and who you become, is your choice. **How you invest your time and energy will ultimately create the world you live in.**

Walk Your Walk

BE STRONG and RISE ABOVE

The world appears to be in chaos, despair, and turmoil right now as the old programming, beliefs, and paradigms are beginning to crumble away. It has been so easy to get caught up in the drama, the judgment, the criticisms; easy to find faults, lay blame, or accuse; easy to drop down into low vibes of fear and despair. **What a waste of your precious energy** when you focus on the problems and the obstacles. STOP IT! **It is time to envisage a world that** is filled with excitement and enthusiasm, where you enjoy living each day doing what you love to do. What would that look and feel like? Connect to those feelings frequently. Sit in the stillness of presence, open your mind and allow the potential of limitless possibilities to present to you. When you silence the chaos, it is easy to see endless possibilities; let your imagination roam free. **REMEMBER –** the outside world is an extension of your inner world. Begin within, create your vision then **IMAGINE LIVING IN IT NOW, FEEL IT** as though it is happening NOW, and the outside world will reflect it back to you. **Because that's how it works.**

SOUL WHISPERS

Ego to Kindness

*Ego cannot rule,
when the truth is the way*

*Ego cannot control actions
when thoughts are pure*

*Ego cannot rule,
when love is the essence of everything you do*

*Be kind when troubles arise
Be kind when in doubt
Be kind when you are angry*

*Kindness begins love
Kindness heals pain
Kindness opens hearts*

*Forgiveness is kindness
Forgiveness is freeing
Forgiveness is Peace*

*Be gentle with yourself
Be gentle to others
Be gentle to nature*

BE AWARE of YOUR VIBES,
EGO is LOW VIBES.
In the outside global world, we are able to witness, from our front row seats, what Ego looks and feels like. Ego exists in the duality world of right and wrong, is easily offended, and goes on the attack if threatened. Ego constantly seeks to be the number one, better than everyone else, more money, more control.
Ego is constantly trying to satisfy a need or want, always searching and seeking outside of itself.
Currently, we are experiencing a lot of ego energy.
SOUL is HIGH VIBES
Our collective purpose is to embrace the higher frequencies of LOVE and JOY.
Our collective purpose is to awaken to higher conscious awareness and live with presence in the present moment fully awake, alert, and aware.
Our collective purpose is to serve and support humanity through kindness and benevolence.
Our collective purpose is to learn, grow, and evolve; to live in balance and harmony; transcend fears to live in a surrendered state of being, and emerge from the old paradigms to the NEW EARTH

Empowering Moments -
WHAT IS YOUR LEGACY? *At the end of this lifetime, when you reflect on your life and see how you have lived and how you have treated people, will that story bring you joy? What is your energetic imprint on this earth? How will you be remembered?*
Write out an epitaph *of who you were and how you wish to be remembered by everyone.*
THEN START LIVING IT.... NOW.
You have to live it, to be remembered for it!

ENERGY IS EVERYTHING – INCLUDING YOU

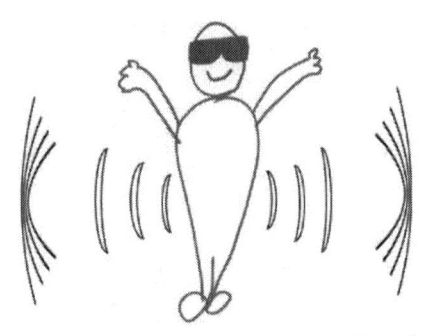

Raise your own Frequency Vibrations

BE PRESENT
*"It is what it is. It is what it is not.
IT IS...full stop"* – Hazel Butterworth

Simply recognize when you are in high or low vibes.
What energy are you infusing into your own reality?
What energy are you meeting every experience with?

Why is it,
that grandma's apple pie always tastes so yummy,
the ingredients are the same as other apple pies?
Answer; Because she makes it with LOVE VIBES.
Have you noticed when you cook, that some days you
are not really" FEELING" like cooking, everything is an
effort, and you are not really fully present, paying
attention, or enjoying the experience? Do you recall
how those meals turned out? Chances are, you were
disappointed. Perhaps the meal looked bland or tasted
bland or you simply ate it without paying any attention.
There was nothing that excited you about the whole
experience. This is so true of life when we are not
present or have no enthusiasm for what we are doing.

Pay attention
BE PRESENT with every experience.

BE FREE of the DRAMA and STORIES
It is easy to be pulled into other people's drama,
stories, perceptions, or beliefs. People can influence
you to take on their beliefs or perceptions of life.
Gossiping is a good example of feeding drama.
I like how Byron Katie teaches
"Your business is none of my business,
My business is none of your business"
Recognize when your emotions are being triggered.
Stories that are being driven by strong emotions and
Ego are often exaggerated or embellished to make the
details or story more dramatic or compelling.
Step out of the drama,
Step out of the story,
Remove the emotions.
= FACT and TRUTH.
Stay with the facts...
that which you experience for yourself, not hearsay,
that which you know to be true, not opinions,
that which is compassion, not judgment,
that which has integrity, not speculation,
that which is your business, not others.
A story may begin with facts,
but then drama and emotions are often added.

ENERGY IS EVERYTHING – INCLUDING YOU

SOUL WHISPERS

TUNE into your SUPERPOWERS

*Everything is Energy, including you.
You are the steps, the dance, the songs that you sing.*

*You are magical, let your magic shine.
Share your magnificence, shine your light bright.
Embrace your brilliance and BE the light.*

*Why is it, when you let your magic shine,
EVERYTHING becomes magical and
life is filled with MIRACLES.?*

*Why is it when you SURRENDER,
when you stop resisting and allow,
life flows easily and effortlessly.*

*Live your dreams, live your life,
love yourself, day and night.*

*Feel the love, feel the vibes
Feel your way through life
and ENJOY the ride.*

*Your life is your legacy
what will yours be?
Awaken, Arrive,
and Arise.*

BE FREE to Be YOU
Nonresistance — Nonjudgement - Nonattachment

Life is not about creating a better version of yourself.
Life is about realizing the magnificence
and brilliance of who you already are.

Life is about awakening to your truth
and liberating yourself to be yourself.

Life is about emerging and evolving
with each and every experience.

Life is about understanding yourself
as you journey through life being
both the participant and the observer
Life is for Living, Loving, Laughing, and Learning.
ENJOY BEING YOU

***Empowering Moments** -*
Your life is your own creation,
consciously or subconsciously.
Ask yourself - What are you creating

BE YOUR SOVEREIGN SELF

**As human beings,
we have the gift of personal freedom
and the liberty of a free mind.
We are light beings navigating this 3D physical
reality, and everything we need is within us.**
We have the freedom of choice, even when
we cannot choose what is happening we can still
choose how we respond to what is happening.
We cannot change the circumstances but
we can change ourselves to navigate through them.
We always have a choice.
Sovereign Self is having the exclusive authority to
choose the direction of your own life and accepting
responsibility for all the decisions you make regarding
your own happiness and well-being.
Sovereign Self, is staying true to your own values
and beliefs, **you are who you "believe" you are.**
It is your own identity that is uniquely you,
that you have sculpted during your life experiences.
Sovereign self is NOT ALLOWING yourself to be
compromised, bullied, forced, coerced, or bribed.
Sovereign Self is standing strong and tall and having
the confidence and freedom to BE YOURSELF.

SOVEREIGNTY IS your Natural State of Being
RECOGNIZE and REMEMBER
You are a light being. You are Energy.

REALIZE
your self-worth and wholeness,
you are the one in charge of yourself,
you are 100% responsible for your energy vibes,
you are 100% accountable for yourself,
your thoughts, words, feelings, and actions,
you have power and are empowered,
Embrace and Go with Flow.

EMBODY YOUR
personal autonomy,
potential and brilliance,
FREE will, and resilience,
Higher Self, and values,
uniqueness and inner gifts,

LIBERATE YOURSELF
from limitations
old paradigms, beliefs
programming, and habits
others' opinions and expectations

AWAKEN
your hearts desires and dreams,
your superpowers,
your intuition and your truth,
your heart to LOVE,
self-determination,
your mind to infinite possibilities,

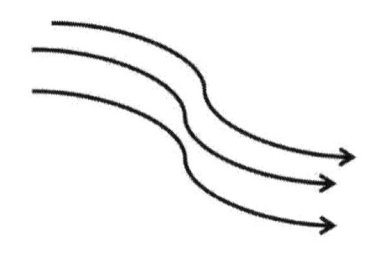

Remember...

ENERGY is EVERYTHING
INCLUDING YOU.

"When ENERGY flows freely

Life flows EASILY"

Choose to live your life

in EASY FLOW.

**"FREE yourself
FROM yourself
FOR yourself"**

HAZEL BUTTERWORTH

Reach for the Stars and the Moon

TUNE INTO YOUR VIBES

TUNE INTO YOUR HEART

TUNE INTO YOUR SOUL POWER

TUNE INTO YOUR SUPERPOWERS

TUNE IN AND TURN UP YOUR VOLUME

"SOUL POWER"
IS YOUR RENEWABLE, SUSTAINABLE, ENERGY-EFFICIENT, PURE, CLEAN, ENERGY SOURCE.

"SOUL KINETICS"
IS THE DYNAMICS OF YOUR SOUL, SPIRIT, HUMAN.

ENERGY is EVERYTHING

INCLUDING YOU

:)

Enjoy

Being YOU.

THE CATALYST

Hazel is often lovingly called "The Catalyst".

Her gentle nudges and persistence help
you to dig deep to discover the gems
that are hidden within you;
open your mind to possibilities
and to realize that you
already have all answers within you.

All this and more as you develop your
Intuition and Sensory Awareness skills.

Many clients and students comment
how calming her voice is,
how her smiles light up the room,
how effective her teaching is, and
how grateful they are
for having her in their life.

To this Hazel smiles, bows, and says
a humble "thank you" from her heart.

*"From my heart to yours
I send you love and light.
Love to comfort and support you.
Light to help see beyond the physical."*

ENERGY IS EVERYTHING – INCLUDING YOU

SOUL WHISPERS

Can be found on the following pages.

13	Who am I?
18	I`m Stuck- I am here on the inside
19	I`m Stuck- Where is the key
30	We are all made of Universal Life Force
31	Who are We?
32	It is what it is
36	The Magic is within you
107	Yesterday is a Memory
164	It`s a Dreamlife
165	It Matters, You Matter
170	Epic Awakenings
172	Realize your own Potential
174	Be Love
180	Inner world, Outer world
184	Ego to kindness
188	Tune into your Superpowers

Soul whispers are intuitive writings that were downloaded during journaling or meditation.

CONCEPTS EXPLAINED

70	ALLOW AND ACKNOWLEDGE ALL EMOTIONS
148	ATTACHMENT AND LABELS
174	BE A KID FOR THE DAY
177	BE AT PEACE
183	BE AWARE OF YOUR VIBES
187	BE FREE TO BE YOU
185	BE FREE OF THE DRAMA
176	BE IN CHARGE OF YOUR OWN ENERGIES
180	BE KIND, BE HUMANE
173	BE LOVE
184	BE PRESENT
181	BE STRONG, RISE ABOVE
42	BE THE CHANGE YOU WANT TO BE
179	BE THE CREATOR OF YOUR WORLD
76	BE THE OBSERVER, WATCH AND LEARN
188	BE YOUR SOVEREIGN SELF
50	BELIEVE IN YOURSELF
136	BELLY BREATHING
116	CATCHPHRASES
132	CENTERING
156	CHINESE MEDICINE, KINESIOLOGY
110	COLLECTIVE CONSCIOUSNESS
109	CONSCIOUS AWARENESS

ENERGY IS EVERYTHING – INCLUDING YOU

144	CREATE THE LIFE OF YOUR DREAMS
161	DREAMS AS MESSAGES
38	EMPOWERING MOMENTS - I CAN
124	EVALUATE THE EQUATION- PARADIGMS
44	EXPLORE AND DISCOVER SELF REALIZATION
102	GREET YOURSELF IN THE MIRROR
130	GROUNDING
14	HAZEL HELP WHY I WROTE THIS BOOK
118	HIDDEN MESSAGES IN WATER
120	HO OPONOPONO
108	I THINK THEREFORE I AM, CONSCIOUS AWARENESS
128	IMPROVE INTERNAL COMMUNICATION, 3 RESERVOIRS
112	INSPIRED INTENTIONS, DON'T NOT NO
150	INTROSPECTION
23	IT IS POSSIBLE TO MAKE SENSE OF THE NONE SENSE
90	LIFE HERE ON EARTH IS TEMPORARY
20	LIFE IS A MYSTERY UNLOCK PIECES OF YOUR PUZZLE
40	LIGHT YOUR OWN FIRE. BECOME YOUR OWN CATALYST
104	LIVE IN THE PRESENT
64	LIVE THE IN LIGHT, WE ARE LIGHT COLOUR SOUND.
54	LOVE EVERY ASPECT OF YOURSELF, ACCEPTANCE
122	MAP OF CONSCIOUSNESS
25	MATCH THE FREQUENCY
96	MIND MOVIES

92	NOURISH ALL ASPECTS OF SELF -VISIBLE/INVISIBLE
160	NUMBERS AS MESSAGES
158	NUMEROLOGY
98	PERSPECTIVES AND PERCEPTIONS
62	RAISE YOUR OWN FREQUENCY, ALL ENERGY IN MOTION
114	RATS EXPLAINED
82	RECONNECT WITH YOUR SOUL
140	REIKI
138	RELEASE AND LET GO
52	RESISTANCE
74	RESILIENCE
28	RESPONSIBILITY
166	SCIENCE IS CATCHING UP
100	SEE WHAT LIFE IS REFLECTING BACK TO YOU
171	SOUL KINETICS
84	SOUL SPIRIT
86	SOURCE SOUL ESSENCE
106	SPEND ENERGY CONSTRUCTIVELY
88	SPIRIT AND HUMAN PHYSICAL YOU
152	STOP EXPECTING PERFECTION - EXPECTATIONS
60	SURRENDER TO THE EXPERIENCE
66	THE FEELGOOD FACTOR
72	THE NEGATIVITY FACTOR
94	THOUGHTS AND EMOTIONS OUTSIDE THE BODY

ENERGY IS EVERYTHING – INCLUDING YOU

46	TIPPING THE SCALES, EVOLVE, EVOLUTION
56	UNCOVERING TRUTHS
146	TRIGGERS
80	UNDERSTAND THE LAWS OF THE UNIVERSE.
58	UNDERSTANDING
68	UNPLEASANT UNWANTED EMOTIONS
164	WE ARE INTERDIMENSIONAL BEINGS
30	WE AR ALL MADE OF UNIVERSAL LIFE FORCE
78	WHO ARE WE, INFINITE BEINGS
154	YIN YANG
48	YOU HAVE THE POWER - LOOK SEE CHOOSE BE

HAZEL BUTTERWORTH

EXPERIENCE MEDITATIONS

FREE meditations are available

on my YOUTUBE channel –

Hazel Butterworth Catalyst for Self Awareness

Or

Visit the link below

https://albertareiki.com/alchemy-of-meditation-videos/

Thank you
for spending time with me as you explored this book.

I would love to hear your feedback,
please share your insights gained.
I invite you to write a review on amazon to help
promote Hazel Help Series.

CONNECT with Hazel

www.albertareiki.com

www.ignitepeacewithin.com

Hazel Help Book Series

Each book has a specific purpose

#1 – Exploring Beyond the Physical
Intuitively sensing Energy bubbles.
The first book is to create awareness
that we are all energy.

FEEL ENERGY – CREATE AWARENESS.

#2 – Everything is Energy, including YOU
When your energy flows freely, life flows easily.
This second book helps to explain that
we are all energy in motion, showing up in
this physical world as unique "Energy" beings.

UNDERSTAND ENERGY – LEARN, DISCOVER.

#3- Empowering Moments
Each and every moment is where the magic begins.
The third book consists of Gentle nudges
to remind you always have choices in every
moment, and that you are your own catalyst.

ACTIONS – WHAT YOU CAN DO FOR YOURSELF.

Printed in Great Britain
by Amazon